Englisch für beruflichen Schulen

2nd edition

Do it! STARTER

von

Elizabeth Hine

unter Mitarbeit der Verlagsredaktion

W0322592

Table of contents

Cornelsen

Auf einen Blick

Do it! Starter ist ein Lehrwerk mit integriertem Workbook für Integrationsklassen, berufsvorbereitende Bildungsmaßnahmen und -kurse. Es dient auch als Wiederholung von grundlegenden Englischkenntnissen auf Stufe A1 des Gemeinsamen Referenzrahmens.

So finden Sie sich im Buch zurecht:

Warm up: Jede Unit beginnt mit einer Einstiegsseite, die kommunikativ in das Thema einführt.

Parts: Auf diesen Doppelseiten werden Anfängerinnen und Anfängern mit geringen Vorkenntnissen elementare Redemittel für Alltag und Beruf, einfache grammatische Formen und sprachliche Grundbausteine vermittelt. Eine große Vielfalt an Differenzierungsaufgaben, die mit diesem Symbol ★ markiert sind und die Sie im Anhang finden, fördern dabei das individualisierte Lernen.

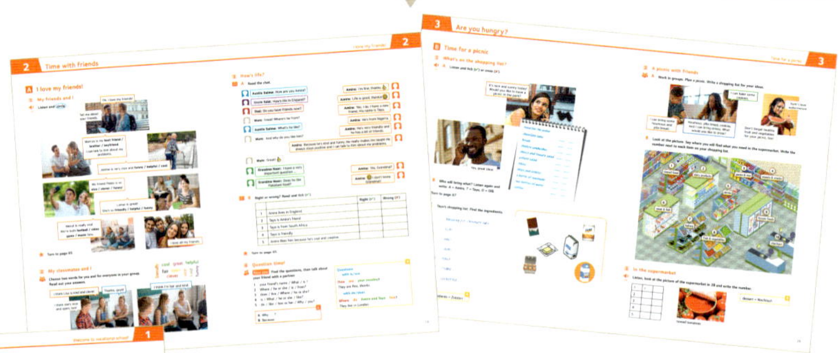

Project: Am Ende einer jeden Unit steht ein handlungsorientiertes Projekt; hier soll mit den erworbenen sprachlichen Fertigkeiten ein haptisches Produkt erstellt werden.

I can do it!: An dieser Stelle kann man den Stoff der zwei vorherigen Units noch einmal wiederholen und festigen.

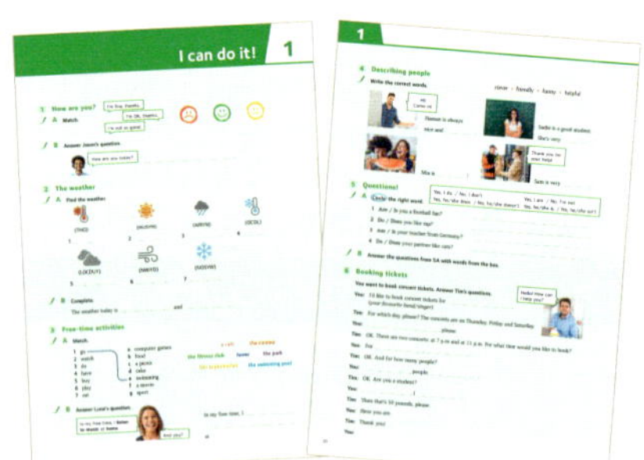

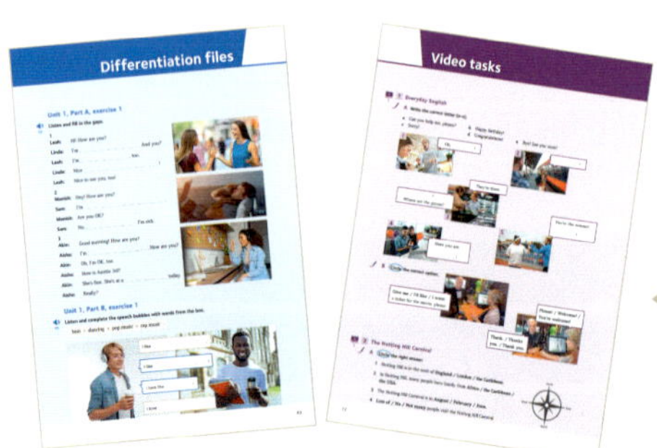

Videos: Kurze Videos beleuchten einzelne Aspekte der Units aus einem anderen Blickwinkel. Übungen dazu sind im Anhang *Video tasks* zu finden.

Anhang: Außerdem finden Sie hier *Differentiation files*, ein Wörterverzeichnis und eine Liste unregelmäßiger Verben.

Die Symbole 🔊 und ▶ verweisen auf die Audio- und Videomaterialien, die Sie in der Lehrerfassung finden.

Lehrerfassung: Die praktische Lehrerfassung des Buches bietet Lösungen direkt auf der Seite und zeigt neue Vokabeln an. Außerdem gibt es viele nützliche Zusatzmaterialien wie Kopiervorlagen und Transkripte, die per Webcode abrufbar sind.

Viel Spaß beim Lernen und gutes Gelingen wünschen Ihnen Autorin und Verlag!

Warm up: Hi!

A **Read.**

Hi! I'm Amira!
I'm from Pakistan.
I live in London,
in the UK.
And you?

Nice to meet you!

B **Now you** **Talk to a partner.**

L

Hi! I'm …
I'm from Afghanistan/Albania/Germany/Iran/Iraq/Nigeria/Romania/Somalia/Syria/Turkey/…
I live in … , Germany. And you? Nice to meet you!

C **Write and circle.**

I'm from ______________________________. I love ______________________________.

football

cooking

shopping

listening to music

sleeping

reading

dancing

watching TV

D **Swap, read and guess who it is.**

Is it Arhan?

No, it isn't.

Is it Nico?

Yes, it is!

A Let's chat

1 How are you?

02 **A** Listen and circle.

1

Hi! How are you?

I'm fine, thanks. / I'm OK, thanks. / I'm not so good.

2

Hi! How are you?

I'm fine, thanks. / I'm OK, thanks. / I'm not so good.

sick = *krank*

3

Good morning. How are you?

I'm fine, thanks. / I'm OK, thanks. / I'm not so good.

★ Turn to page 63.

B Now you Talk to a partner.

A How are you?
B I'm … … fine, thanks. ☺ … OK, thanks. 😐 … not so good. ☹ L

Small talk topics

weather ✓	politics ✗
music ✓	health ✗
sport ✓	religion ✗

In the UK, people talk about the weather a lot. And in your country?

Video 1
Watch the video and look at page 72 for more practice of everyday English.

2 The weather today

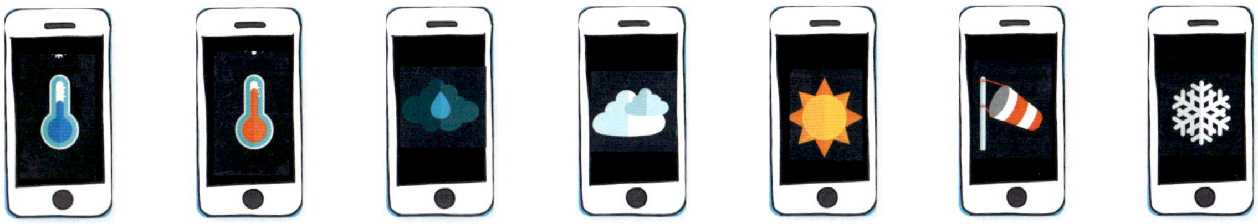

cold hot rainy cloudy sunny windy snowy

A Listen and match.

03

1 Brrr! It's so **cold**!

2 I love **sunny** days!

3 It's so **hot** today!

4 I hate **rainy** weather!

5 Oh no! It's **cloudy**!

6 It's a bit **windy** today!

7 Yay! It's **snowy**!

a

d

e

b

f

c

g

B Look out of the window. Write.

It's ____________, today. / It's ____________ and ____________ today.

C Listen and complete.

04

Cem: What's your favourite weather?

Tina: I love ____________ and ____________ weather. And you?

Cem: I love ____________ and ____________ weather!

Tina: You're crazy, Cem!

D Now you Talk to a partner.

L

A What is your … ?
B I like/love … weather. And you?
A I …

B What do you like?

1 Nice to meet you

05 Listen and complete.

★ Turn to page 63.

2 Free time

Match the words and pictures.

~~animals~~ ▪ cooking ▪ football ▪ music ▪ shopping

1 ________

2 ________

3 ________

4 *animals*

5 ________

3 Hot or cold?

06 **A** Listen and read.

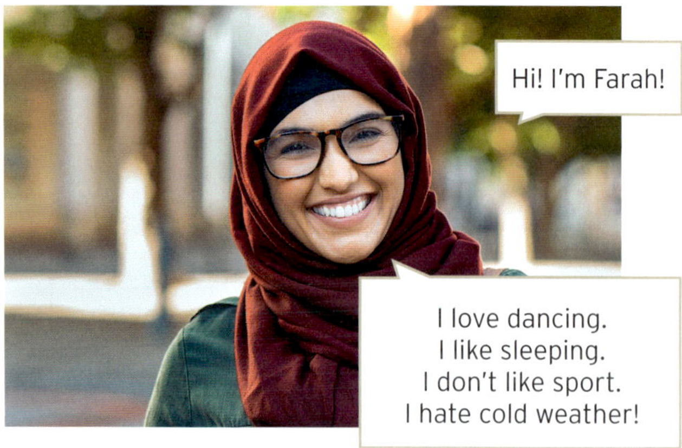

B Listen and complete. 07

★ Turn to page 64.

C Write about you.

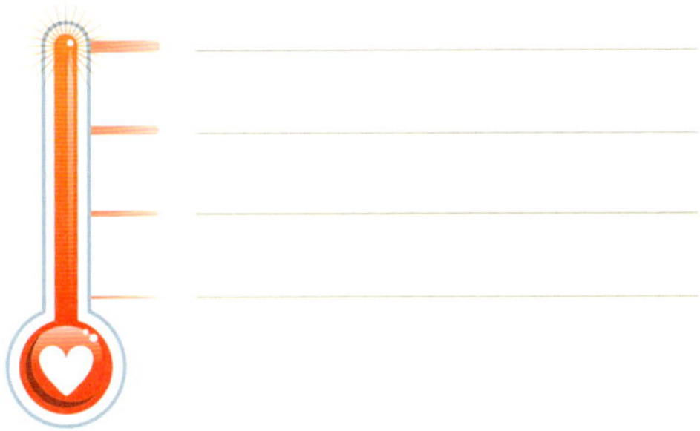

D **Now you** Talk to a partner.

L

A Do you like ... ?
B Yes, I do. I love ... ! /
No, I don't. I hate ... !
And you?

4 A sunny day

A Read the comic.

B Circle.

The weather is **cloudy** / **sunny** / **rainy**. Amira and Farah go to the **café** /**park** / **restaurant**. Olli and Tayo **listen to music** / **play football** / **dance**. Amira and Farah love the **park** / **weather** / **song**. Amira loves pizza and Olli loves **music** / **pizza** / **cooking**, too!

★ Turn to page 64.

C Welcome to vocational school!

1 At the secretary's office

08 **A Listen and read.**

1 Good morning! Can I help you?

2 Good morning! I'm a new student.

3 Welcome to vocational school! Please sit down.

4 Thank you.

5 What's your name?

6 It's Amira Ali.

7 Please spell it.

8 It's Amira: A-M-I-R-A. Ali: A-L-I.

9 Thank you.

B Now you Talk to a partner.

L

A Good morning. / Good afternoon. What's your name?
B It's …
A Please spell that.
B It's …
A Thank you.

2 Student registration

registration = *Anmeldung*

09 **A Listen and match.**

1 What's your address?
2 And your postcode?
3 What's your telephone number?
4 Do you have an email address?
5 Good luck, Amira!

a Thank you.
b It's 25 Green Road, London.
c It's E5 6AH.
d It's 07892 86145.
e It's amira@webnet.nex.

B Complete the form for Amira. Then read it with a partner.

Name: ______

Address: ______ **Postcode:** ______

Telephone number: ______

Email address: ______

~~Green Road, 25~~ ✘
25 Green Road ✔
@ = at
.com = dot com

★ Turn to page 64.

3 What's your name?

Do the role-play.

Secretary	Student
Good … . Can I help you?	Good … . I'm a new student.
Welcome to … ! Please sit down.	Thank …
What's your name?	It's …
Please spell it.	It's …
What's your address?	It's …
Do you have an email address?	Yes, I do. It's …
Thank you and good … !	…

4 Time to relax!

Read. Then listen and complete. 10

★ Turn to page 64.

5 What would you like?

Now you **Talk with a partner.**

L

A What would you like?
B A … and a … , please.
A Here you are. Are you a student?
B Yes, I am. / No, I'm not.
A That's … pounds, please.

Project: My class

11 **A** Listen and tick (✔).

Name	summer	winter	cat	dog	café	park	coffee	tea
Lara								
Ben	✔							

Your ideas!

B Talk with a partner. Tick (✔).

Name	summer	winter	cat	dog	café	park	coffee	tea		

C Make a poster.

Time with friends

Warm up: My perfect day

12 **A Listen and read.**

This is my perfect day.

The weather is hot and sunny!

I drink a nice cup of tea in the morning.

I eat my favourite food!

I hang out with my friends in the afternoon.

I relax in the evening.

B Write three sentences.

On a perfect day, the weather is …

______________________________ .

I ______________________________ .

______________________________ .

L

- sunny/rainy/snowy/…
- (to) do sport
- (to) listen to (pop/rap/…) music
- (to) go to the park/café/…
- (to) watch TV
- (to) play computer games / football/…
- (to) sleep all day

C Work in a group. Guess, then count your points.

1 I think the weather is rainy.

2 No, it isn't. Sorry. Zero points!

3 I think the weather is snowy and sunny.

4 Yes, it is. One point for you!

5 I think you play basketball.

6 Yes, I do. One point for you.

7 I think you relax at home.

8 No, I don't. Sorry.

L

A How many points do you have?
B I have … points.
A Who's the winner in your group?
B It's Güler.

A I love my friends!

1 My friends and I

13 Listen and circle.

Oh, I love my friends!

Tell me about your friends.

Marcus is my **best friend / brother / boyfriend**.
I can talk to him about my problems.

Janine is very nice and **funny / helpful / cool**.

My friend Pablo is so **nice / clever / funny**!

Lamai is great!
She's so **friendly / helpful / funny**.

Mesut is really cool.
We're both **football / video game / music** fans.

I love all my friends.

Turn to page 65.

2 My classmates and I

Choose two words for you and for everyone in your group.
Read out your answers.

friendly cool great helpful fair open clever nice kind funny

I think Lisa is kind and clever.

Thanks, guys!

I think she's nice and open, too!

I think I'm fair and kind.

3 How's life?

A Read the chat.

Auntie Saima: How are you Amira?

Amira: I'm fine, thanks.

Uncle Said: How's life in England?

Amira: Life is good, thanks!

Dad: Do you have friends now?

Amira: Yes, I do. I have a new friend. His name is Tayo.

Mum: Great! Where's he from?

Amira: He's from Nigeria.

Auntie Saima: What's he like?

Amira: He's very friendly and he has a lot of friends.

Mum: And why do you like him?

Amira: Because he's kind and funny. He really makes me laugh! He always stays positive and I can talk to him about my problems.

Mum: Great!

Grandma Noor: I have a very important question ...

Amira: Yes, Grandma?

Grandma Noor: Does he like Pakistani food?

Amira: I don't know, Grandma!!

B Right or wrong? Read and tick (✓).

		Right (✓)	Wrong (✗)
1	Amira lives in England.		
2	Tayo is Amira's friend.		
3	Tayo is from South Africa.		
4	Tayo is friendly.		
5	Amira likes him because he's cool and creative.		

★ Turn to page 65.

4 Question time!

Now you Find the questions, then talk about your friend with a partner.

1 your friend's name / What / is ?
2 Where / he or she / is / from?
3 does / live / Where / he or she?
4 is / What / he or she / like?
5 do / like / him or her / Why / you?

L

A Why … ?
B Because …

Questions

… with *is/are*

How are your cousins?
They are fine, thanks.

… with *do/does*

Where do Amira and Tayo live?
They live in London.

B What do you do with your friends?

1 Where is it?

Listen and match. 14

___ café _1_ cinema ___ fitness club ___ park

___ stadium ___ supermarket ___ swimming pool

L: I think number one/two/... is a ...

2 What do you do there?

A Find six activities.

(to) work out

watchamoviehaveapicnicgoswimminggotoaconcertdrinkcoffeeworkoutbuyfood

B **Now you** Talk with a partner.

You drink coffee at a ...

3 Olli chats to his cousin Vicky

A Right or wrong? Listen and tick (✔). 15

		Right (✔)	Wrong (✘)
1	Olli speaks to his cousin Vicky.		
2	Tayo is from Germany.		
3	Tayo plays the guitar.		
4	Tayo sings rock songs.		
5	Nadima cooks Syrian food for Olli.		
6	Olli doesn't play chess with Vicky.		

chess

★ Turn to page 65.

B **Now you** **Check with a partner.**

Number one/two/… is right/wrong.
Tayo isn't … . He's …
Tayo sings … . He doesn't sing …
Nadima doesn't cook … . She cooks …

☺ Tayo loves pop music.
☹ He doesn't like rap.
☺ Nadima likes chess.
☹ She doesn't like cooking.

4 Game: True (✓) or false (✗)?

Play in groups. Choose two true sentences and one false sentence.

never = *nie, niemals*
sometimes = *manchmal*
always = *immer, ständig*

sleep for more than nine hours
get up before 6 a.m.
listen to very loud music
talk on the phone for more than one hour
talk in my sleep
sing in the shower
smoke shisha
talk to my pet/cat/dog/other animals
spend too much money on clothes
eat really spicy food
watch TV all day

5 Ice cream is always a good idea

Read the comic. Complete the sentences.

always ▪ fitness club ▪ never ▪ sport

Amira and Olli want to go to the ____________ , but Farah doesn't want to do ____________ . She ____________ wants to do sport. Tayo is very happy. He thinks that ice cream is ____________ a good idea!

★ **Turn to page 66.**

C I'd like to book a table

Days of the week

Monday
Tuesday
Wednesday
Thursday
Friday
Saturday
Sunday *the weekend!*

1 Do you have time on Saturday at 8 p.m.?

16 **A** Listen and circle.

1

2

3

★ Turn to page 66.

B **Now you** Make a date to meet a friend.

A Do you want to … ? / Let's … go to the cinema / go out for dinner / play tennis / …
B Yes, good/great idea!
No, I don't. I'd like to … / Let's …
A What about Monday/Tuesday/… at … a.m./p.m.?
B Yes, that's fine.
Sorry, I can't. What about … at … ?

2 A birthday dinner

A Read and find the words.

It's Amira's birthday on ______________ . She wants to go to a ______________ .

B Listen and write. 17

Mamma Italia. Josie here. How can I help you?

Mamma Italia — Table 3 — Monday / Tuesday: closed

		Wednesday	Thursday	Friday	Saturday	Sunday
6 p.m.	Name:				Sue Jones	
	How many?				2	
	Phone number:					
7 p.m.	Name:	Ken Chan				Bob Lindon
	How many?	5				4
	Phone number:	01895 63471				0203 47926
8 p.m.	Name:					Jesse Tay
	How many?					3
	Phone number:					07643 28304

C Work with a partner. Match the questions and answers.

1 How can I help you?
2 For which day, please?
3 And what time?
4 For how many people?
5 What's your name, please?

a For five people.
b I'd like to book a table.
c It's Ali, Amira Ali.
d Saturday, please.
e Seven p.m.

D Now listen and check. 17

★ Turn to page 66.

3 Please leave a message

Listen and complete the form in 2B. 18

4 Dinner with friends

A **Now you** Make a booking. Leave a message on a student's phone.

This is Abu Said restaurant. Please leave a message.

L

Hello. / Good morning/afternoon/evening.
I'd like to book a table for … people on … at … p.m.
My name is … . My number is … . Thank you.

B Phone the customer and confirm or change the booking.

This is … from Abu Said restaurant. Your table is booked for … at … . Thank you.

This is … from Abu Said restaurant. I'm sorry, our restaurant is full on … / at …

Project: My favourite person

A Listen and read. Then match the photos to the speech bubbles. (19)

Number one is photo …

a

b

c

d

1 My favourite person is my son, Shan. I'm from China, but he's from England. He's five years old. He's my favourite person because he's clever and kind.

Ying

Walid

2 My favourite person isn't a person. It's an animal, my cat Tiger. I'm from Syria, but my cat is from England. I love Tiger because she's nice and funny! She's lazy, like me!

3 My favourite person is my big sister, Dika. She's 22 years old. We're both from Croatia. Dika is my favourite person because she's always kind and helpful.

Mila

Leroy

4 My favourite person is my friend Simón. Simón comes from Colombia, but he lives in London, too. I like him because he's friendly and open.

B Now you Work with a partner. Talk about Shan, Tiger, Dika and Simón.

L

He/She comes from … . / He/She's from …
He/She's … years old.
He/She's nice/funny/… and …

C Write about your favourite person.

D Present your favourite person to your group.

1 How are you?

A Match.

I'm fine, thanks.

I'm OK, thanks.

I'm not so good.

B Answer Jason's question.

How are you today?

______________________________ .

2 The weather

A Find the weather.

(THO)

1 _ _ _

(NUSYN)

2 _ _ _ _ _

(AIRYN)

3 _ _ _ _ _

(OCDL)

4 _ _ _ _

(LOCDUY)

5 _ _ _ _ _ _

(NWIYD)

6 _ _ _ _ _

(NOSYW)

7 _ _ _ _ _

B Complete.

The weather today is ____________________ and ____________________ .

3 Free-time activities

A Match.

1	go	a	computer games
2	watch	b	food
3	do	c	a picnic
4	have	d	cake
5	buy	e	swimming
6	play	f	a movie
7	eat	g	sport

a café, the cinema, the fitness club, home, the park, the supermarket, the swimming pool

B Answer Luna's question.

In my free time, I **listen to music** at **home**.

And you?

In my free time, I ______________________

____

at ______________________________ .

4 Describing people

Write the correct words.

clever ▪ friendly ▪ funny ▪ helpful

Hassan is always nice and ______________ .

Sadie is a good student. She's very ______________ .

Mia is ______________ !

Sam is very ______________ .

5 Questions!

Yes, I do. / No, I don't.	Yes, I am. / No, I'm not.
Yes, he/she does. / No, he/she doesn't.	Yes, he/she is. / No, he/she isn't

A Circle the right word.

1 **Are / Is** you a football fan? ______________________________ .

2 **Do / Does** you like rap? ______________________________ .

3 **Am / Is** your teacher from Germany? ______________________________ .

4 **Do / Does** your partner like cats? ______________________________ .

B Answer the questions from 5A with words from the box.

6 Booking tickets

You want to book concert tickets. Answer Tim's questions.

You: I'd like to book concert tickets for ______________________ .
(*your favourite band/singer*)

Tim: For which day, please? The concerts are on Thursday, Friday and Saturday.

You: ______________________ , please.

Tim: OK. There are two concerts: at 7 p.m and at 11 p.m. For what time would you like to book?

You: For ________________ , ________________ .

Tim: OK. And for how many people?

You: ________________ people, ________________ .

Tim: OK. Are you a student?

You: ________________ , I ________________ .

Tim: Then that's 50 pounds, please.

You: Here you are.

Tim: Thank you!

You: ______________________________ .

Are you hungry? 3

Warm up: Eating good food

A Find the words.

C	A	R	R	O	T	X	G	L	B
Y	W	M	A	P	P	L	E	E	A
T	O	M	A	T	O	Z	S	M	N
L	R	O	Q	T	T	B	P	O	A
P	U	N	P	E	A	S	A	N	N
E	X	I	K	F	T	E	Q	H	A
A	C	O	G	P	O	Y	R	B	I
R	V	N	O	R	A	N	G	E	K

B Match the foods to the picture.

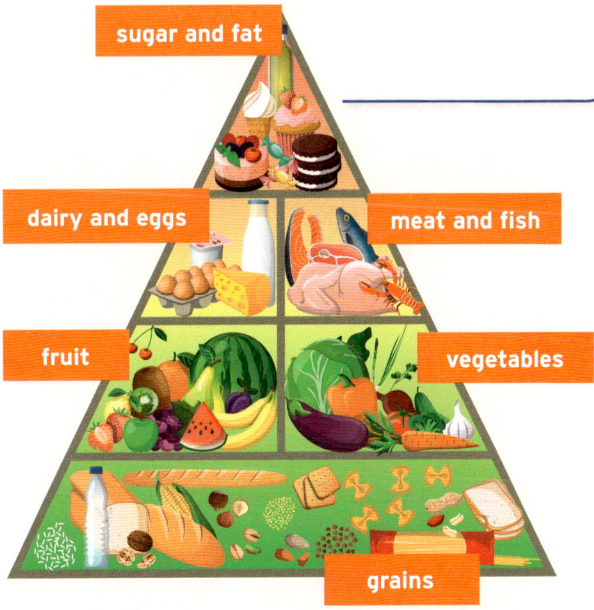

bread cheese cucumber oil cake cookies milk beef kiwi lamb rice melon yoghurt grapes butter pork cream chicken strawberries chocolate garlic pasta potatoes aubergine (red/green/yellow) peppers

I love hamburgers!
A hamburger with salad is healthy, right?!

healthy = *gesund*

C **Now you** Talk with a partner.

A How often do you eat … ?
B I always eat … / I eat … every day.
I sometimes/never eat …
I'm a vegetarian/vegan.

A Do you eat … ?
B I eat a lot of / too much …
I need to eat more …
I think my diet is OK / (not so) healthy.

A My favourite food

1 Amira's favourite food

20

A **Listen and read.**

Croatian
Syrian
Nigerian
Turkish
German
Italian
Chinese
Polish
British
Indian
food
Brazilian
Spanish
South African
Afghan
Russian
Romanian
Albanian

B **Now you** **Talk to your partner. Write the answers.**

L

A What's your favourite food?	**B** My … / I …
A Do you like cooking?	**B** No, I don't. / Yes, I do. I like cooking …
A What's your best dish?	**B** My …

C **Talk about your partner.**

♂ he – his   he/she/it + -s
♀ she – her

2 How does it taste?

21

Listen and write.

salty ▪ sour ▪ spicy ▪ sweet

I'm thirsty! This food is too ______________ !

Wow! These chips are really ______________ !

Wow! These donuts are so ______________ !

It's so ______________ !

3 Food from home

A Talk about the photos.

a

b

c

d

L
In photo … , I can see rice/…
I think this is food from …
I (don't) think it's spicy/…
The food in photo … looks tasty 👍 /
doesn't look tasty 👎.
I would like to eat it because it looks …
I wouldn't like to eat it because it's too …

B What food do they miss from home? Listen and match the photos in exercise 3A to the people.

22

(to) miss = *vermissen*

☐ 
Katja

☐ 
Chris

☐ 
Yaa

☐ 
Basam

C Read, listen and circle.

22

1 Katja comes from Germany, but she lives in **England / Spain / Sweden**. She misses German **bread / sausage / cheese**. She doesn't eat **vegetables / rice / meat**.

2 Chris comes from **Scotland / the USA / India**, but he lives in Brazil. He misses **Scottish / Indian / Thai** curry. His favourite dish is **chicken / fish / vegetable** curry with rice and Indian **cheese / sauce / bread**.

3 Yaa comes from Ghana, but she lives in **Germany / Scotland / India**. She misses jollof **rice / curry / sauce**. She eats it with fish and **lemon / orange / banana**.

4 Basam comes from **Ireland / Italy / Iraq**, but he lives in Canada. He misses food like houmous, falafel and kebab with mint **tea / coffee / chocolate**. He says, "Iraqi food in Canada doesn't **look / taste / smell** the same."

★ Turn to page 67.

D Now you Talk in a group.

L
In … (country) people eat a lot of …
… food is tasty/spicy/…
The most popular dish in … is … with …
My favourite dish in Germany/… is …

I miss sweet *bundi laddu* from Pakistan.

What food from your country do you miss?

B Time for a picnic

1 What's on the shopping list?

23 **A** Listen and tick (✓) or cross (✗).

Food for the picnic

chocolate cake	___	___
bread	___	___
chicken sandwiches	___	___
cheese and tomato salad	___	___
potato salad	___	___
olives	___	___
chips and cookies	___	___
a bottle of lemonade	___	___
two bottles of water	___	___
coffee	___	___

23 **B** Who will bring what? Listen again and write: *A* = Amira, *T* = Tayo, *O* = Olli.

★ Turn to page 67.

C Tayo's shopping list: Find the ingredients.

Shopping list: Chocolate cake

KLIM _ _ _ _

GGES _ _ _ _

UGARS _ _ _ _ _

FOULR _ _ _ _ _

TTUBRE _ _ _ _ _ _

COCHOTALE _ _ _ _ _ _ _ _ _

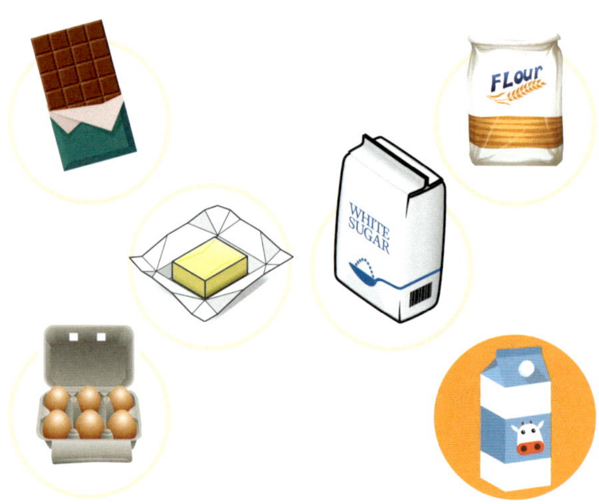

ingredients = *Zutaten*

2 A picnic with friends

A Work in groups. Plan a picnic. Write a shopping list for your ideas.

B Look at the picture. Say where you will find what you need in the supermarket. Write the number next to each item on your shopping list.

3 In the supermarket

Listen, look at the picture of the supermarket in 2B and write the number.

24

1	7	
2		
3		
4		
5		

tinned tomatoes

dessert = *Nachtisch*

C Time to go shopping

1 Money around the world

£: pounds and pence

$: dollars and cents

€: euros and cents

A **How much is it? Count.**

1 It's ____________ pounds.

2 It's ____________ pounds and ____________ pence.

1 notes

2 coins

B **Now you** **Talk with a partner.**

Which notes and coins do you have in your country?

In my country, we have 5, 10 ... euro/ afghani/leu ... notes.

In my country, you can find 10, 20 ... cent/ afghani/bani coins.

25

C **Listen and circle the right price .**

1 €50.10 / €10.50 / €55

2 £7.25 / £17.50 / £25.70

3 $29.50 / $19.25 / $5.90

4 AU$54 / AU$52 / AU$32

How to say it

£1.50 = one pound fifty / one pound and fifty pence

€20.75 = twenty euros seventy-five / twenty euros and seventy-five cents

$120 = one hundred and twenty dollars

★ **Turn to page 67.**

2 Special offers

Read the flyer.

Fresco's special offers for you this week!

All fresh vegetables half price!

500g packets of rice – 2 for 1!

Time to bake! 25% off flour, sugar and eggs!

Great! A supermarket flyer! Special offers! We can save money!

half price = 50% cheaper
£2 = £1

25% off = 25% cheaper
25% off £100 = £75

2 for 1
= buy one, get one free (= £0)

3 How much is it?

A Read and circle.

Tayo: Let's buy some bread for the picnic.

Amira: Yes, good idea.

Tim: Hi! **How can I help you? / Do you need help? / What do you want?**

Tayo: The baguettes look tasty.

Amira: Yes, **how much money / how many / how much** are the baguettes?

Tim: One baguette is one pound ten pence.

Amira: **I'd like / I want / Give me** three baguettes.

Tim: Three? OK, That's three pounds thirty.

Amira: Sorry. **I can't hear you. / Could you repeat that? / Say it again!**

Tim: Three pounds thirty pence, please.

Amira: Here you are.

Tim: Thank you. **Have a nice day! / See you later! / Go away!**

Amira: You, too! Bye!

26 **B** Listen and check.

★ Turn to page 68.

4 How can I help you?

A Work with a partner. You are shop assistants. Make a poster of your products and prices.

B Work in groups of four. Present your shop to the other pair.

C Now you Go shopping with your partner. (A = shop assistant; C = customer).

L

A How can I help you?
C Do you have … ?
A Yes, we do. Here you are. / No, we don't. Sorry.

C How much is/are the … ?
A It's … / They're …
C I'd like …
A That's …

Project: Let's cook!

A Match the instructions to the photos.

a Add pepper.
b Bake for 20 minutes.
c Boil the potatoes.
d Cut the onions.
e Fry the onions.
f Mix the eggs and flour.

B Work with a partner. Put the instructions into the right order.

It's time to cook!
This is how you can make the best vegetable curry in the world!

Ingredients
3 potatoes
2 carrots
1 cauliflower
100g of frozen peas
2 onions
curry powder
1 can of tomatoes
400 ml of vegetable stock
(= Gemüsebrühe)
yoghurt (if you like)

frying pan

Instructions

- [1] Cut, then boil the potatoes and vegetables.
- [ ] Eat your curry with yoghurt, if you like.
- [ ] Fry the onions, then add the curry powder.
- [ ] Put oil into a pan.
- [ ] Add the vegetables and cook all the ingredients for 5 minutes.
- [ ] Add the tomatoes to the onions and cook for 2–3 minutes; then add the vegetable stock.
- [ ] Cut the onions.

C Put the photos into the right order. Then find the food.

Mix the ingredients.

Throw it into the air and catch it.

Warm up the pan.

Put the mixture into the pan.

Ingredients: 300 ml sunflower oil ▪ 100 g flour ▪ 2 eggs ▪ a pinch (= *Prise*) of salt

This is a recipe for (APNKACES) ____________________ .

D Choose a dish. Write a list of ingredients and instructions.

L
The ingredients are 1/2 can(s) of tomatoes/peas/… , two onions/carrots/… , …

Eating and celebrating 4

Warm up: Pancake day!

27 **A** **Listen and match the photos.**

a

b

c

d

e

f

g

h

B **Work in groups. Talk about the pictures in A.**

L

I think people eat these pancakes in Austria/Canada/Ethiopia/France/Germany/India/Japan/Russia/Turkey / the UK / the Ukraine / the USA.

I think they're sweet. You probably eat them with fruit/jam / maple syrup / honey/sugar/ …
I think they're savoury. There's probably cheese/spinach/caviar/… inside.
There are probably noodles/vegetables/raisins/... inside.

They look sweet/savoury/spicy/…
I would/wouldn't like to try them because …

sweet ≠ savoury

(strawberry) jam

tasty/delicious

raisins

maple syrup

C **Talk about pancakes in your country.**

My friend Rahul and I love pancakes! Our favourite filling is lemon juice and sugar!

And you? What pancakes do you eat in your country?

What are your favourite fillings?

In Brazil, we have *panquecas*.

My favourite filling is chicken with tomato sauce.

4 Eating and celebrating

A Celebrating all year round

1 My year

A Put the letters in the right order and find the missing months.

January

July

April

October

NUJE
GUASTU
YAM
RHCMA
REBEMPETS
CEBMEDRE
RUARYBEF
VONBEREM

28 **B** Listen and check.

2 Festival time!

A Work in groups. Read and match the texts to the photos on page 31.

1 In English-speaking countries like the UK, USA and Australia, ***Christmas*** is on the 25th December. Many people have a tree at home with lots of colourful decorations on it. They put presents under the tree.

2 The ***Notting Hill Carnival*** is at the end of August in Notting Hill, London. It is a festival of Caribbean culture, music and food. People wear colourful costumes and there is a big street parade.

3 ***US Independence Day*** is on the 4th of July. On this day, the USA celebrates independence from Britain. There are street parades and fireworks. Many people have picnics or barbecues in a park or in the garden at home. You can see the colours of the flag everywhere: red, white and blue!

4 ***Halloween*** is on the 31st October. People wear scary costumes and go to parties. Many people cut a face into a pumpkin and put a candle inside!

5 ***St Patrick's Day*** is a festival from Ireland. It is on the 17th of March. There are street parades and people wear green clothes and hats. Musicians play traditional Irish music and people dance and sing.

6 ***Bonfire Night*** is a festival in the UK, on the 5th November. There are big bonfires and people come to eat and drink around them. You can watch fireworks in the park or in your garden at home.

(to) celebrate = *feiern*   face = *Gesicht*   independence = *Unabhängigkeit*   scary = *gruselig*

barbecue

bonfire

candle

fireworks

tree

In Australia, Christmas is in summer and we have beach parties!

B Work in pairs. Listen and write the festival. Which pair has the most correct answers?

29

1 ______ 2 ______

3 ______ 4 ______

5 ______ 6 ______

C Listen and circle.

30

My favourite festival is in **spring / autumn / winter**, on the 31st of **January / March / December**. It's New Year's Eve. We say 'bye' to the old year and 'hello' to the new year! I usually have a **barbecue / party / parade** with my friends. We wear funny **hats / clothes / T-shirts**! We eat tasty food, then we listen to music and dance! At midnight, we go and watch the **TV / fireworks / show** in the street.

Video 2

Watch the video and look at pages 72 and 73 to learn more about the Notting Hill Carnival.

★ Turn to page 68.

D **Now you** Talk about your favourite festival.

A What's your favourite festival?
A When is it?
A What do you eat?
A What do you do?

B My favourite festival is Eid/Hanukkah / New Year / …
B It's in spring/…/March/…
B We eat meat/vegetables/fish with potatoes/rice/…
B We eat special food / wear … clothes / …
We get presents/…
In the evening/… , we dance / go to …
People sing/watch … / have a picnic / …

B Celebrating Holi with a friend

1 True or false?

A Work with a partner. Read, then choose: true (✔) or false (✘).

My friend Rahul comes from India, but now he lives in Dublin, Ireland.

We **went** to a Holi festival. It **was** great!

Last year, I **visited** him.

> **Every year**, I **visit** Rahul. *(Präsens)*
> **Last year**, I **visited** Rahul. *(Vergangenheit)*
>
> We always **go** to a Holi festival **in March.** *(Präsens)*
> We **went** to a Holi festival **last March.** *(Vergangenheit)*
>
> Holi **is** a festival. *(Präsens)*
> The festival **was** great **yesterday**. *(Vergangenheit)*

Holi is the Indian festival of spring and colours. It is in March. People throw colour powder and water.

People from India live all around the world. That's why you can celebrate Holi in many countries. Everyone can join in the fun!

colour powder

There **was** a big Holi street party in the centre of Dublin.

We **played** with colour powder and water.

It **was** a lot of fun!

	True (✔)	False (✘)
1 Rahul is Amira's friend.	___	___
2 He lives in London, England.	___	___
3 Amira visited Rahul last year.	___	___
4 Rahul and Amira went to a music festival.	___	___
5 There was a street party in the centre of the city.	___	___
6 They played with colour powder and pumpkins.	___	___
7 Amira didn't like the festival.	___	___

B Correct the false sentences.

> L
> A Number is … true.
> B Yes. But number … is false.
> Rahul lives in … , not in …

> like ≠ don't like *(Präsens)*
> like**d** ≠ **didn't** like *(Vergangenheit)*

2 How was your day yesterday?

31 **A Listen and put the photos in the right order (1–7).**

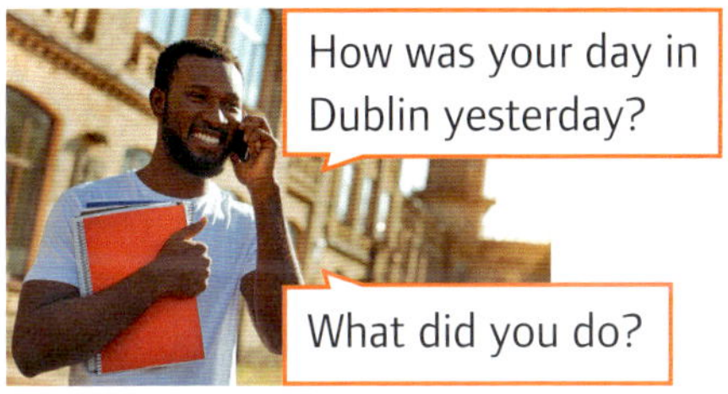

River Liffey

Dublin Castle

Irish stew

B Work with a partner. Check your answers.

L

Number one/two/… is: They ate Irish stew for lunch / bought a coffee / did a boat trip / visited Dublin castle / walked next to the river / watched TV / went shopping.

Turn to page 69.

3 What did you do yesterday?

A Work in groups. Write three things you did yesterday on three pieces of paper.

I met my friend in a café.

B Mix the pieces of paper. Read out loud.

C Guess. Who is it?

C A weekend in the Lake District

1 Do you want to come with us?

Read and answer the questions.

1 Where does Rahul want to go? He wants to go to …

2 Who does he want to go with? He wants to go with …

3 When does he want to go?

The Lake District is the biggest national park in England. There are 16 lakes!

Rahul: Hi!

Amira: Hi!

Rahul: Do you want to come to the Lake District with me and my friends? For a weekend?

Amira: When?

Rahul: In June.

Amira: 👍👍👍

2 Where would you like to stay?

A Read and circle A, B or C.

Send

From: rahul@email.nex

To: Friends

Subject: Places to stay

Hi guys

I found some nice places to stay in the Lake District. Look at the document. Which place do you like best?

See you soon!

Rahul

Which sentence is correct?

a Rahul wrote an email to his friends. He wants to find a place to stay.

b Amira wrote an email to Rahul. She doesn't want to go to the Lake District.

c Rahul wrote an email to a hotel. He wants to book a room.

single room | double room | private bathroom | shared bathroom | breakfast | free WiFi | parking

B **Read about Amira and Rahul's perfect holiday. Then choose a place to stay for them.**

My perfect holiday is in a small town or the countryside, but no tents – it's too cold! I want to sleep in a nice bed, but I don't have a lot of money, so nothing too expensive. I want to see some culture, maybe an old town or a museum, too. And of course, I want to try the local food – yum!

My perfect holiday is to be close to nature. Then I can really relax. I don't need to go out to restaurants, and I'm happy to cook my own food. I also love meeting different people on holiday and making new friends. It's OK to spend a bit more money on the right place – it's important to really enjoy your time on holiday.

Hotel Panorama ***
Your home in the centre of a beautiful old town!
Comfortable rooms and full room service.
Try our traditional English breakfast (£12/person).
Cafés and restaurants 5 minutes away
£50/per night £80/night
All rooms with a private bathroom. FREE WIFI P

Lakeside B&B **
Come and enjoy the family atmosphere in our home near the lake!
Only 10 minutes to the lake by car or a beautiful 30-minute walk.
Start the morning with a traditional English breakfast or cornflakes, toast and homemade jam. Home-cooked evening meals (£10–15/meal).
£30/night £50/night
All rooms with a private bathroom. P FREE WIFI

The Traveller's Hostel
Enjoy nature and meet people from all around the world!
Only 20 minutes by bus or car to the lakes or to a small town with cafés and restaurants.
8 people, 4 bunk beds: £14/per person/night
£22 per person/night
Shared bathrooms, TV room; two large kitchens

Campsite By-the-Lake
Sleep next to the lake!
Wake up next to the lake!
£10/person/night
Shared toilets and showers
Small camp shop selling food and drink
Bonfire area by the lake

L
I think Amira/Rahul would like … because …
I don't think Amira/Rahul would like … because …
I think they should stay at … because …

C **Now you** **Talk to your partner.**

Where would you like to stay?

I'd like to stay at the Hotel Panorama / … because … And you?

3 Booking a place to stay

32 Listen and circle or write.

Booking form

Number of people: 2 / 3/ 4

Number of rooms: 1 / 2 / 4

Dates: 5th–7th / 12th–14th / 19th–21st of June

Number of nights: 1 / 2 / 3

Name: Rahul G __ __ __ __

Phone number: __7 __ __ 5 8 __ 4 9 __

Saying the date

1st	the first	10th	the tenth
2nd	the second	20th	the twentieth
3rd	the third	21st	the twenty-first
4th	the fourth	30th	the thirtieth
5th	the fifth	31st	the thirty-first

★ Turn to page 69.

4 How to get there

33 Which is it? Listen and write the correct word.

1 ______ 2 ______ 3 ______ 4 ______ 5 ______

bike

bus

car

train

plane

5 Taking the train

34 **A** Listen and complete with numbers from the list.

1 ▪ 07 ▪ 10 ▪ 12 ▪ 15 ▪ 21

Video 3

Watch the video and look at page 74 to learn more about booking train tickets and accommodation in English.

Train departures

Time	Destination	Platform
11:45	Oxford	____
____:02	London Paddington	5
13:23	Watford	____
14:____	Manchester	13
14:43	Liverpool	____
15:____	Birmingham	7

Saying train times

09:15: nine fifteen
12:30: twelve-thirty
15:45: fifteen-forty-five
11:06: eleven 'oh'-six
20:33: twenty thirty-three

(to) depart = *abfahren*
departure = *Abfahrt*
destination = *Ziel*
platform = *Gleis*

B **Now check your answers with a partner. Read your answers out loud.**

L

The 11:45 (*eleven forty-five*) train to Oxford will depart from platform … .
The …:02 (*oh two*) train to London Paddington will depart from platform 5.

Turn to page 69.

C **Read and find the right train for Amira. How much is it? Read your answers out loud.**

Amira is at vocational school until 1 p.m. on Fridays. She wants to arrive before 8 p.m.

Friday, 12th June
London Euston Station to Oxenholme Lake District Station

Departs	Arrives
13:54	17:10
17:26	21:23
18:15	22:08

Prices

Adult	Student	Child (under 16)
£90.50	£60.32	£45.20

L

The best train for Amira departs at … and arrives at … .
It's … .

D **Work with a partner. Find the right train and price.**

1

Susie and Ranjit want to depart at about 5.30 p.m. They need one adult ticket and one student ticket.

2

Nele isn't a student. She wants to travel with two children. She wants to arrive before 9 p.m.

3

Luis is a student and Sandra works until 5.30 p.m. They want to travel with one child.

Project: A weekend in London

A **Work in groups. Plan a weekend in London.**

Our weekend in London!

- *Place to stay for two nights*
- *One activity for Saturday during the day / in the evening*
- *Place for dinner*
- *+ one extra activity (you can look on the internet!)*

Budget: £180 per person

People in London call the underground train system the *Tube*. A ticket for one day costs about £13.

Places to stay

Hotel Victoria

Stay in the exciting centre of London!

Walking distance to most attractions

£70 person/night, with breakfast

East End Hostel

Stay in the cool East End of London!

20 minutes by Tube to the centre of London

£40 person/night, with shared kitchen

Holiday apartment

Your home in the city!

Clean and with everything you need! 45 minutes by Tube to the centre of London

£100/night

Things to do

Bus tour

See the most important places in an original old London bus!

3 hours, £30 per person

London Eye

See London from the sky! Take beautiful photos from the top!

30 minutes, £25 per person

Buckingham Palace

Come and see this beautiful palace and say hello to the Queen!

£30 per person

Dinner

Indian restaurant

Come and try the UK's favourite food: curry!

£15/person

Takeaway: fish and chips

Try this traditional British dish!

£10/person

Cook at home

Relax and cook 'at home'!

£5/person

B **Present your weekend to the class.**

L

We want to stay in …
During the day, we want to do a bus tour / go on the London Eye / visit Buckingham Palace.
For our extra activity, we want to visit/walk/go/do/ …
For dinner, we will go to an Indian restaurant / eat fish and chips / cook … at home.

1 Let's eat!

A Find 12 food words.

chocolateapplebeefcheesebreadpeaspastachickenbananacakemilkcarrot

B Write the words from A in the table.

sugar and fat	dairy	meat	fruit	vegetables	grains

2 Do you like spicy food?

A Ebo and Diep talk about food. Complete the sentences with words from the box.

No ▪ Yes ▪ I do ▪ I don't ▪ I am ▪ I'm not ▪ Yes

spicy

tacos

Ebo: Do you like spicy food, Diep?

Diep: ____________ , ____________ , Ebo. My favourite food is Mexican food. I love chicken tacos with extra chilli! And you? Do you like spicy food?

Ebo: ____________ , ____________ . Chilli is too spicy ! My favourite food is falafel with rice.

Diep: Yum! Falafel with rice … and lots of chilli! … Are you hungry?

Ebo: No, ____________ . Are *you* hungry?

Diep: ____________ , ____________ ! I want to eat falafel now!

B Look at 2A. Circle the right option.

Diep **like** / **likes** spicy food. **Her** / **His** favourite food is chicken tacos. She **are** / **is** hungry.

Ebo **don't like** / **doesn't like** spicy food. **Her** / **His** favourite food is falafel with rice.

He **aren't** / **isn't** hungry.

3 I'd like to order some food

A Choose the right option. Write the number (1–5).

1 Would you like
2 How much
3 please
4 That's
5 How can I

Matt: Hi! ☐ help you?

Lily: ☐ is the feta cheese salad?

Matt: It's €5.

Lily: OK. One feta cheese salad, ☐ .

Matt: ☐ a drink?

Lily: Yes, please. A coke.

Matt: A coke is €1.50. OK. A feta cheese salad and a coke. ☐ €6.50, please.

feta cheese salad

B Look at the prices in A. Circle the right options.

One feta cheese salad is **five** / **fifteen** / **fifty** euros. A coke is **fifteen cents** / **one euro fifty** / **one hundred and fifty euros**. A feta cheese salad and a coke is **six euros fifteen** / **six euros and five cents** / **six euros fifty**.

4 When is it?

Circle the correct season. Then answer Mei's question.

My birthday is on the 17th of July.
It's in **spring / summer / autumn / winter.**

And you? When's your birthday?

My birthday is on the ______________

of ______________ .

It's in ______________ .

5 Where did you go?

A Match the questions and the answers.

1 Where did you go last summer?
2 What did you see?
3 Where did you stay?
4 Where was your hostel?
5 What did you eat?
6 What did you do?

a I stayed in a hostel.
b I ate fish and chips and curry.
c I went shopping.
d I went to London.
e It was in the centre of London.
f I saw Buckingham Palace and Big Ben.

B Answer Jamal's question.

Last weekend I visited my friend Rob and we went to a party.

And you? What did you do last weekend?

I ______________

____

______________ .

Working life 5

Warm up: Where do they work?

35

A Listen to the noises and say the jobs.

B Match the jobs and places of work. Read your answers out loud.

1 carer
2 cashier
3 cook
4 mechanic
5 postal worker
6 taxi driver
7 waiter/waitress

a car repair shop
b car
c bike or van
d kitchen
e supermarket
f restaurant
g care home

a/an
Before consonants (**b**, **c**, **d**, etc.) = **a**
a cleaner / **a** factory
A taxi driver drives **a** taxi.

Before **a**, **e**, **i**, **o**, **u** = **an**
an assistant / **an** office
An office worker works in **an** office.

! Vicky is **a** **p**olice officer.
! Liam is **an** **E**nglish teacher.

C Play with a partner. Choose a job from the picture. Find your partner's job. Ask questions.

L

Questions	Answers
Do you work in a factory / a laboratory / a care home / an office / … ? Do you work with people/children/customers/money/tools/ … ? Do you sell/make/paint/test/clean/repair … things/places? Do you drive a car/van?	Yes, I do. / No, I don't.
Are you a tradesperson / an office worker / a driver / … ?	Yes, I am. / No, I'm not.

tradesperson = *Handwerker/in*
(to) drive = *fahren*; driver = *Fahrer/in*
(to) paint = malen; painter = *Maler/in*

tools

van

lorry (*UK*) / truck (*USA*)

5 Working life

A Where do you work?

1 A clown works in a circus

Find the jobs in the word snake and match them to the photos.

carerhairdressermechanicofficeworkersalesassistantwaiter

1

2

3

4

5

6

2 What do they do?

A Work in groups. Complete the mind map for *waiter/waitress* with words from boxes A and B.

A bring ▪ check ▪ cook ▪ cut ▪ dry ▪ file ▪ fry ▪ help ▪ repair ▪ serve ▪ take ▪ talk to ▪ type ▪ wash

B cars ▪ customers ▪ documents ▪ engines ▪ food & drinks ▪ hair ▪ letters ▪ meat & vegetables ▪ payment ▪ people

waiter/waitress

bring
serve food
talk to

B Now choose one more job. Complete a mind map for the job. Read your ideas to the class. Which group has the most ideas?

3 What would you like to do?

colleague = a person you work with
old ≠ young   older ≠ younger

A Read, listen and circle the right words.

36

I don't like working with **colleagues / computers / customers** and I'm not so good at organizing things, so I don't want **a factory / an office / a shop** job. I'm good at working with my hands, so I want to do something practical. I'd like to work with **cars / food / tools** and make things!

I don't like cold weather, so I don't want to work outside! I'm not good at selling things or working with **cars / children / money**. I'd like to work independently, but with nice **colleagues / customers / tools** and of course a nice boss! I'm good at **organizing / painting / repairing** things and working on the computer, so I'd like an office job.

I'm good at looking after people and helping them to feel **bad / good / happy**. I'm not very good at working with my hands, so I wouldn't want to be a painter or a **factory / laboratory / metal** worker! I'd like to work with older **animals / children / people** because they can tell me interesting stories about their lives.

★ Turn to page 70.

B Work with a partner. Choose jobs for Tayo, Amira and Rahul.

L
I think … would like to be a … because he/she likes …
He/She is good at / not so good at …

C **Now you** Complete the sentences on a piece of paper.

I like working with … (computers/customers/people/ …).
I'm good at … (working with tools/customers/computers/my hands/ …).
I'm not so good at … (organizing/talking/helping/…).
I'd like to work … (in an office/a restaurant/a hotel/a care home/on a construction site/ …).

D Work in groups. Swap pieces of paper and read out loud. Guess who it is.

B A part-time job

1 Amira's first day at work

A Work with a partner. Read the cartoon. Put the pictures into the right order.

part-time job = < 30 hours/week

full-time job = > 30 hours/week

Excuse me, please. = *Entschuldigen Sie, bitte.*

(to) miss the bus = *den Bus verpassen*

(to) spill = etwas *verschütten*

left ←

B Put the sentences into the right order.

___ She ran out of the house. She wanted to know the time. So she asked a woman.

___ Then she ran to the bus stop. But she missed the bus. She was very stressed.

_1_ In the morning, Amira didn't hear her alarm clock. So she got up late.

___ Then she found the room and met her new boss. Amira was nervous, but her boss was nice.

___ She saw the bus stop and started to run. But … Oh no! She spilled coffee on a man's T-shirt.

___ She arrived at the company offices, but she couldn't find Room 25. So she asked a man.

C Listen and check. Read the correct answers out loud. 37

D Game. Play in groups. Answer your teacher's questions. The fastest group with the right answer gets one point. The group with the most points is the winner.

L
Because she couldn't find …
Yes, she did. / No, she didn't.
Yes, he was. / No, he wasn't.

Viele Verben in der Vergangenheit enden mit *-ed*, z.B. ask – ask**ed**; want – want**ed**.

Aber nicht alle! > Irregular verbs, page 86

Präsens	*Vergangenheit*	*Präsens*	*Vergangenheit*
buy	**bought**	run	**ran**
get up	**got up**	say	**said**
find	**found**	see	**saw**
meet	**met**	sleep	**slept**

2 Yesterday

A Amira tells Tayo about her bad day. Complete the text with words from the box.

asked ▪ bought ▪ didn't see ▪ got up ▪ ran ▪ slept ▪ was ▪ ~~wasn't~~

It was my first day at my new job and it _wasn't_ a good day! I ________ for too long and I didn't hear my alarm clock! I ________ really late – at 8.30! I didn't have time for breakfast at home. So I ________ a coffee to drink. Then I ________ a woman what the time was. It was 9.10. I was *really* late! So I ________ to the bus stop. And then I ________ a man and I spilled coffee on his T-shirt! I ________ very stressed!

B Now listen and check your answers. 38

C Now you Write about your day yesterday.

I ________ at ________.

Then I ________.

I ________.

It ________ a good day!

3 Asking for help and saying sorry

39

A Look at the photos and listen. Then find the right words in the speech bubbles.

1 (XCEEUS EM) ____________ , where is reception, please?

3 Oh no! I'm (ROSYR) ____________ !

4 Good morning. I'm Tim. Sorry I'm (ATEL) ____________ !

2 Excuse me, what's (HET MTIE) ____________ , please?

blouse  serviettes 

(to) understand = *verstehen*

straight on ↑ right →

39

B Listen again. True (✔) or false (✘)? Correct the false information.

	✔	✘	
1 The reception is straight on and on the right.	___	___	____________
2 The time is two thirty.	___	___	____________
3 The customer had a new blouse.	___	___	____________
4 The waitress offered her a free tea.	___	___	____________
5 Tim was late because he missed the train.	___	___	____________

★ Turn to pages 70–71.

4 Do you have a part-time job?

Now you **Work with a partner. Talk about part-time jobs.**

L

A Do you have a part-time job?
A Where do you work?
A Do you like your job?
A Why do/don't you like it?

B Yes, I do.
B I work in an office / a restaurant/factory/…
B Yes, I do. / No, I don't.
B Because my boss/colleagues are/aren't nice. / Because it's boring/interesting. / Because I like / don't like working with …

A Do you have a part-time job?
A Where would you like to work?
A Why would you like to work there?

B No, I don't.
B I'd like to work …
B Because I like working with … / Because I want to earn money. / Because I want to do work experience in …

C Tuesday afternoon in the office

1 A tour of the office

Tuesday afternoon at work was much better.
I met my colleague, Mike. He was very helpful.

Hi. I'm Mike.
Nice to meet you.

I'll show you the office.
Come with me.

40

A Listen and find the things and places. Write the numbers (1–6) on the plan.

1 Mike's desk
2 Amira's desk
3 photocopier
4 stationery cupboard
5 toilets
6 kitchen

L
Mike's desk **is** number …
The toilets **are** number …

corner

photocopier

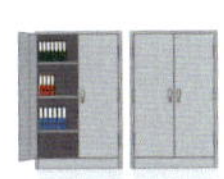
cupboard

stationery = things you need for writing, e.g. paper, pens, etc.

Amira's new office

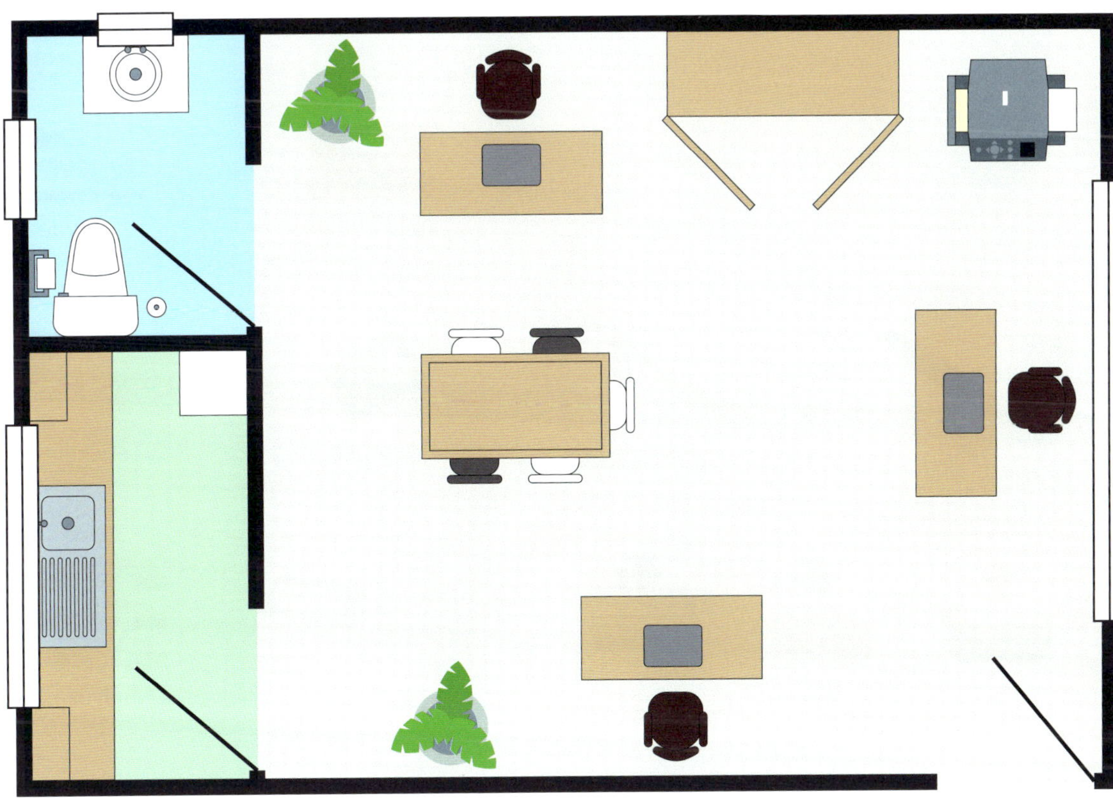

B Work in groups. Play a game. One person chooses a classroom thing. The rest of the group find out what it is.

Things in the classroom

board | chair | teacher's desk | plant | window

pencil case | pen | book | bag | jacket

1 Is it on the left, next to the window?

2 No, it isn't. Sorry.

3 I know! Is it on the right, next to the window? Is it the cupboard?

4 Yes, it is! It's the cupboard!

Where's the … ?

The desk is next to the window.

2 In the stationery cupboard

A 41 Mike helps Amira find things in the stationery cupboard. First read the words below the pictures. Then listen and write the numbers.

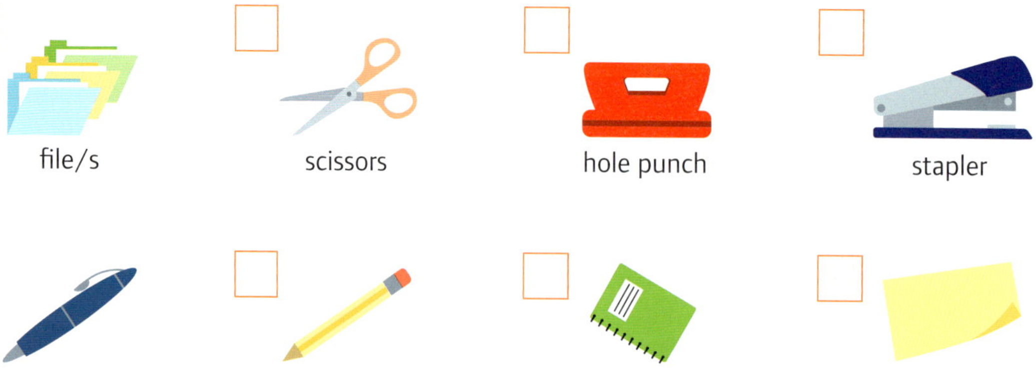

☐ file/s ☐ scissors ☐ hole punch ☐ stapler

☐ pen ☐ pencil ☐ notepad ☐ sticky notes

in | on | under

key | shelves

B **Work with a partner. Read and write the names on the right box. Which box is empty?**

The pens are on the top shelf in the brown box.

The pencils are in the yellow box next to the pens. On the right.

The notepads are on the middle shelf under the pens.

The scissors are on the bottom shelf.

The files are next to the notepads, on the left.

The hole punches are in the blue box on the right of the notepads.

The staplers are on the top shelf, next to the pens. On the left.

The sticky notes are in the red box next to the scissors. On the left.

3 My ideal office

A **Draw your ideal office here or on a piece of paper. Don't show it to other students!**

Your office needs: a kitchen, toilets, a photocopier, your desk and a stationery cupboard.

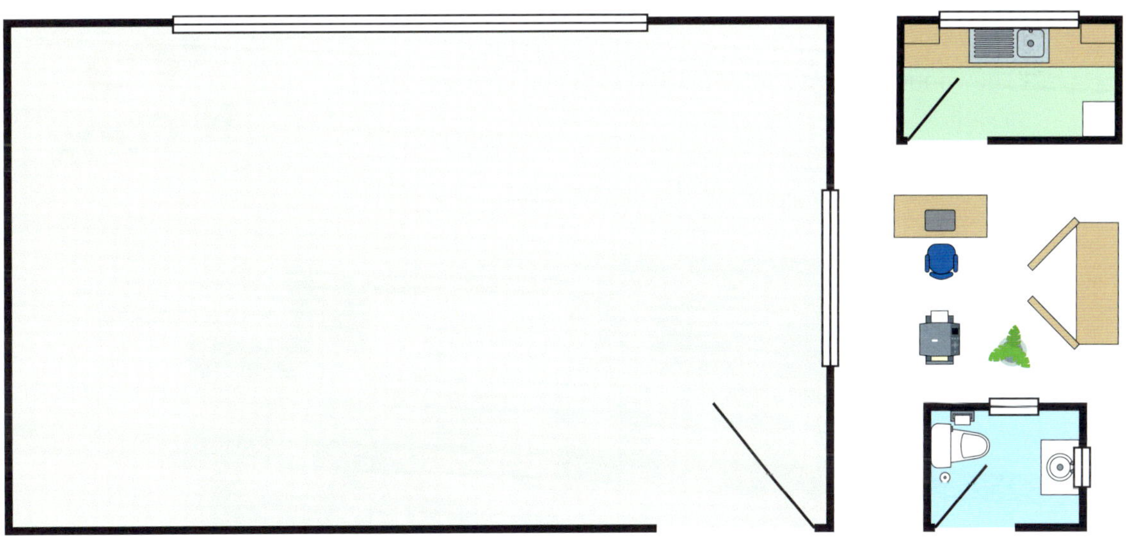

B **Work with a partner. Ask questions and draw your partner's office on a piece of paper. Don't look!**

A Where's your desk / the kitchen / … ? **B** It's on the left/right / in the right/left corner / next to the …	**A** Where are the toilets? **B** They are …

C **Now look at both offices. Which picture is the most correct?**

Project: The job skills game

Work in a small group. Make a job skills game for jobs that you know.

A Choose four jobs per person from Unit 5 (or your own ideas).

B Make a card for each job. Think about the job and the skills you need to do the job. Put the skills in order (1–5).

COOK

SKILL LEVEL

You need to be good at …

looking after people:	2
organizing things:	4
working with a computer:	1
working with customers:	3
working with your hands/tools:	5

C Put all your cards in the centre of the table with the jobs on the top.

D Play the game.

1 Everyone starts with four cards.
2 The youngest person chooses one skill, e.g. organizing things.
3 Everyone looks at the top card and says the number.
4 The person with the most points is the winner. He or she takes the top card from everyone in the group.
5 The winner looks at his or her top card and chooses a skill.
6 Do 3–5 again.
7 The winner of the game has the most cards.

How many points do you have?

I have 5 points.

You have 5 points? You're the winner this time!

E Now give your cards to another group. Play again.

Warm up: What will you do in the holidays?

42 **A Listen to the interviews. Match the people to their plans for the summer.**

Amira

Rahul

Tayo

Olli

Farah

a I'll visit a friend in Italy.

b I'll start an apprenticeship.

c I'll get a job.

d I'll stay at home and relax.

e I'll do an internship.

Apprenticeship/Internship

An **apprentice** does an **apprenticeship.** He/She works for a company, usually for 2–4 years, to learn practical skills for a job. Apprentices often go to vocational school or college, too.

An **intern** does an **internship**. He/She works in a company to get experience (= *Erfahrung*) in that job. Internships are usually 2 months to 2 years long. People often do an internship in the summer holidays or when they finish school or college.

L Congratulations! = *Herzlichen Glückwunsch!*

B Work in groups. Talk about what you think the person next to you will do in the next holidays.

Use ***will*** to talk about the future.

I **will** / I'**ll** go on holiday.
She **will** / She'**ll** get a job.
He **will** / He'**ll** do an internship.

will not = won't
Will you work this summer?
No, I **won't**. I'**ll** relax at home.

A Looking for an internship

1 Amira and Tayo's plans

A Listen and circle the correct information. 43

Tell me more about your apprenticeship, Tayo.

1 Tayo is happy because he'll start **an apprenticeship / an internship / a job** soon.

2 He'll work in **a factory / an office / a workshop**.

3 After the apprenticeship, Tayo will be a **mechanic / metal worker / tailor**.

4 He'll start his apprenticeship next **month / week / year**.

5 Amira will **do an internship / go on holiday / start a job** in the summer.

(to) worry = to think about a problem a lot: *Don't worry, be happy!*
busy = when you have a lot of things to do and not much time to relax

Turn to page 71.

B Work in a group. Look at the links on page 53 and answer the questions.

1 In which position/s will the intern work with:

… children? ____________

… clothes ____________

… computers and a photocopier? ____________

… customers/guests? ____________

… equipment? ____________

… food? ____________

… patients? ____________

… tools? ____________

2 Which positions are part-time? ____________

3 Put the positions in order from the longest to the shortest time.

longest — shortest

____ ____ ____ ____ ____ ____ ____ ____ ____

Tayo found an apprenticeship. I'll try to find an internship now!

department store = *Kaufhaus*
future = *Zukunft, zukünftige*
employment opportunities = *Berufschancen*
equipment = *Ausrüstung*
medical = *medizinisch*
experience = *Erfahrung*
position = *(Arbeits-)Stelle*
exciting = *aufregend*

https://www.opportunities.nex/interships

Opportunities for vocational school students in London

1 **Billy's Car Repair Shop: interns wanted**
Learn important technical skills in a busy car repair shop. Future employment opportunities. 14 months, full-time.

2 **CC Hotel: internship: reception**
3-month internship opportunity at a modern hotel in the centre of the UK capital city! You will learn about working with guests and hotel administration. 35 hours per week.

3 **Looking Good Fashion Stores: interns needed**
Do you want to gain experience in a tailor's workshop? Then come and do an internship with us! You will do practical work helping our tailors to do different tasks. 25 hours per week, 9-month internship.

4 **Four Trees Care Home: internship opportunity**
On-the-job training in our friendly care home. You will learn about the medical and social needs of our patients. Three years, full-time.

5 **SPT Laboratories: internship opportunity**
Summer internships for vocational school students. Prepare and assist with experiments and research in our modern laboratories. 2 months, 20 hours per week.

6 **Ristorante Mamma: internship: pizza baker**
Come and join our young and motivated team! You will learn about traditional Italian ways to make pizza and hygiene standards in a working kitchen. Kitchen experience needed. 6 months, part-time.

7 **Happy Kids Kindergarten: motivated intern needed**
One year internship opportunity at our friendly and caring kindergarten. Opportunities for future employment. Childcare experience needed. 18 months, full-time position.

8 **PLM Construction: internships offered for painters, construction workers and other trades**
Opportunities for motivated young people who want an exciting future in construction. No experience needed, but you must be fit, want to learn and work in a team. One year, 35–40 hours per week.

9 **Workway Office Equipment: interns wanted**
Interns needed for 8-month (part-time) internships. You will help manage a busy office and communicate with customers.

C **Now you** Talk about internships.

Yes, I would. I'd like to do an internship in a kindergarten because I love kids! And you, Kate?

No, I wouldn't. I'd like to do an apprenticeship on a construction site because I like working with tools.

Would you like to do an internship, Walid?

B Job skills

1 Looking at job ads

44 **A Listen to Tayo's questions. Circle the right word.**

1 What's the name of the **manager / company / city**?

2 **What / When / Where** is the internship?

3 For how many **months / weeks / years** is the internship?

4 Which **activities / jobs / tasks** will the intern do?

5 **How / When / Where** do you apply for the internship?

job ad = *Stellenanzeige*
(to) apply for a job = *sich auf eine Stelle bewerben*
task = *Aufgabe*

★ Turn to page 71.

B Work in groups. Choose one job ad from page 55. Complete Tayo's questions from 1A, then find the information to answer them.

1 What's the name of the ______________ ?

____

2 ______________ is the internship?

____

3 For how many ______________ is the internship?

____

4 Which ______________ will the intern do?

____

5 ______________ do you apply for the internship?

____

Applying for an internship

CV (*UK*) / resume (*USA*) = *Lebenslauf*
application = *Bewerbung*
application form = *Bewerbungformular*
cover letter = *Bewerbunsgsschreiben*
(job) interview = *Vorstellungsgespräch*
(to) gain experience = *Erfahrung sammeln*

C Now you Talk in your group: Which internship would you apply for? Why?

I'd apply for the internship at the hotel / restaurant / office suppliers because …
… I'd like to work with customers / food / … / in a hotel /a restaurant / an office.
… I'd like to do an internship for … months / years.
… I'd like to learn about …

1 **CC Hotel**

Internship opportunity: Three-month internship in our hotel reception

- July–September, full-time, 35 hours/week
- A modern hotel in the centre of London
- For vocational school students, age 16–19. You should be friendly and communicative.
- You will work at our reception desk and welcome our guests. You will give them the information they need and answer questions. If they want to do any activities in London, you will make bookings and help them with transport, etc. You will help with any problems and make our guests happy!
  You will also learn to work with our online hotel booking system and answer emails about bookings.

If you're interested, please send your CV and cover letter to Sara Patel: s.patel@cchotel.nex

2 *Mamma Italian Restaurant*

Do you love Italian food? Do you want to help our guests to enjoy the Italian experience in our restaurant with the best pizzas outside Italy?

Then come and join our friendly team!

We need an intern to help in our busy kitchen. You will learn how to make delicious, traditional Italian pizza and all the skills you need to work in a restaurant kitchen. We would like to find an intern who has some kitchen experience and is motivated, hard-working and can work under pressure.

The internship is for 6 months, part-time (about 15 hours per week). Possible employment opportunities.

If you're interested, please phone Sandro Altobelli to arrange an interview on: 020 73962

3 **3 Come and join the Workway team!** WORKWAY OFFICE SUPPLIERS LTD

About Workway

We are one of the UK's leading office suppliers. We supply offices all around the UK with the equipment they need: from stationery to desks and photocopiers.

Our internships

We need 3 interns to help our office team. The internship is for 8 months, part-time (about 20 hours per week). Interns will learn about the most important administrative tasks in our busy office and work with customers.

If you are organized, communicative and enjoy working in a team, then please complete our online application form here.

communicative = good at talking to people
can work under pressure = a person who stays cool when he/she is very busy and needs to work quickly
hard-working = you can work a lot and you aren't lazy
motivated = you really want to work and learn

2 My strengths

A Work with a partner. Match the people and the speech bubbles.

strengths = your best personal qualities, what you are good at

Adu, waiter

Lang, carpenter

Jack, kindergarten teacher

Kim, hairdresser

a In my job, it's very important to be communicative and friendly. It's also important to be creative and learn different styles.

b You need to be enthusiastic because you need a lot of energy to do this job! And you should be patient, because little kids have to learn a lot of things!

c It my job you need to be able to work under pressure! You also need to be polite and friendly to all customers.

d For my job, you need to be practical because you will need to use different tools quickly and safely. It's also important to be physically fit.

caring = a person who is nice and likes to help people
enthusiastic = a person who is always happy and excited about jobs/tasks
patient = a person who doesn't get angry if a person doesn't do what he/she wants
practical = a person who is good at working with his/her hands
physically fit = a person with a healthy and strong body
punctual = a person who is never late

B Look at the word cloud. Choose one more strength for each job.

physically fit, punctual, creative, friendly, practical, can work under pressure, patient, flexible, caring, **strengths**, enthusiastic, organized, motivated, good at teamwork, communicative, want to learn

C Answer Amira's question. Write.

I am ______________, ______________

and ______________.

I am organized, friendly and punctual. What are your personal strengths?

C Applying for a job

1 Writing a cover email

(to) introduce yourself = *sich vorstellen*
(to) look forward to = *sich auf etwas freuen*

A Work with a partner. Read and match. Write the correct letter (a–f).

You write a cover email or letter to:
- introduce yourself
- say why you are interested in the position
- tell the company about your skills

☐ **1** Start your e-mail with: (♀) *Dear Ms Patel, …* or (♂) *Dear Mr Patel, …*
If there isn't a contact name in the ad, write: *Dear Sir or Madam, …*

☐ **2** Say where you saw the job advert, e.g, on a website, in a newspaper, on a notice board (*schwarzes Brett*).

☐ **3** Introduce yourself: say what you are doing now and why you want the job or internship.

☐ **4** Talk about your relevant strengths and/or experience.

☐ **5** Say that you are sending your CV and that they can contact you for more information.

☐ **6** Say that you look forward to hearing from the person soon.

Send | From | To | Subject

a *I am hard-working and organized. Last year, I worked in a hotel in Germany.*
b *My CV is attached (email) / enclosed (letter). Please contact me if you have any questions.*
c *Dear Sir or Madam,*
d *I saw your ad on my school "Jobs" notice board.*
e *I look forward to hearing from you soon.*
f *My name is Tamir Yilmaz and I am a student at a vocational school in Berlin. I would like to gain experience working with patients in a care home.*

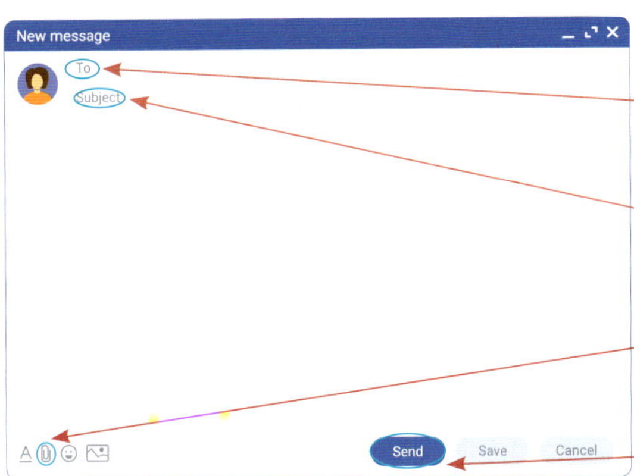

Writing an application email

To: Write the email address of the company contact person here.

Subject: Say what the email is about, e.g. *Application: internship/job/apprenticeship*

Click here to attach your document (e.g. CV).

Send: Send your application – good luck!

B **Work with a partner. Read the parts of Amira's cover email to Sara Patel at CC Hotel. Put the parts into the right order. Write the numbers 1–7.**

From	amira@webnet.nex
To	s.patel@cchotel.nex
Subject	Application: Internship at CC Hotel

Send

☐ I look forward to hearing from you.

☐ I saw your ad on the opportunities.nex website. I would like to apply for the internship position at your hotel.

☐ Dear Ms Patel,

☐ My name is Amira Ali and I am a student at a vocational school in London. I would like to gain experience with your international guests and learn how to use a hotel booking system.

☐ I am polite, reliable, enthusiastic and willing to learn.

☐ Yours sincerely,
Amira Ali

☐ My CV is attached. Please contact me if you have any questions.

CV **Amira Ali**

Contact details

________________: 25, Green Road, London E5 6AH

Telephone ______________________: 07895 86145

Email address: amira@webnet.nex

____

20.. – now: Vocational school, London

20.. – 20..: Barnet High School, London

____

July 20..: Part-time office assistant, Keystores Ltd
Tasks: email correspondence, typing letters, making client appointments

20.. – 20..: Part-time waitress, Jolly's Diner
Tasks: taking customer orders, serving food

____

Excellent computer and administrative skills.

Experience working with ____________________.

Languages: ______________________. Urdu (native speaker), German (basic knowledge)

2 Writing a CV

(to) make an appointment = make a date to meet or speak to a person
basic knowledge = you know a little bit
language: e.g. German, English, Turkish, …
native speaker = *Muttersprachler/in:* you are a native speaker if it is your first language, e.g. *My parents are from Turkey, but we live in Germany. My native languages are Turkish and German.*

Complete Amira's CV on page 58 with words from the box.

Address ■ customers ■ Education ■ English ■ number ■ Skills ■ Work experience

3 A job interview

(to) invite = *einladen*
(to) confirm = *bestätigen*

Send | To: amira@webnet.nex
Subject: Application

Dear Ms Ali,

Thank you for your application.

I would like to invite you to a job interview on Friday, 12th May at 11 a.m.

Please confirm the appointment.

I look forward to meeting you.

Yours sincerely,
Sara Patel

45 **A Listen to Amira's job interview. Say if the sentences are true (✔) or false (✘).**

	✔	✘
1 Sara asks Amira about her experience with customers.	___	___
2 Amira likes working with customers because she likes chatting to people.	___	___
3 Amira says that she is always punctual and motivated.	___	___
4 Amira would like to work with computers when she finishes vocational school.	___	___
5 Sara will call Amira next week.	___	___

B Work with a partner. Correct the false sentences.

46 **C Listen and circle and complete the correct answers.**

1 Did Amira get the internship? Yes, ______________ . No, ______________ .
2 When should Amira come to the hotel? On the ______________ of ______________ .
3 What does Tayo say? ______________ ! That's ______________ news! Let's celebrate!

6 Starting an internship

Game: What will the future bring?

A **Read Amira's predictions.**

These are my predictions for the future.

In five years' time, I think I'll ...

... have a good job in a hotel.

... learn to play the guitar.

... buy a cool old camera and take great photos!

prediction = what you think will happen in the future

B **Sit in groups. Write three predictions about the future on three pieces of paper. (Don't show the group).**

Write: *In five years' time, you will (have a good job / ...)*

be a millionaire / have lots of money	speak very good (English/...)
buy a car / ...	be a famous (footballer / movie star / ...)
have a partner / children / a pet / ...	live in a flat/house/villa
learn to play the ... / speak ...	travel to ...
be a kindergarten teacher / metal worker / ...	be happy/healthy/...

C **Put your papers in the middle of the table and mix them.**

D **Everyone takes three pieces of paper. Read your predictions to the group. Say if you think they will happen or not.**

I think this will happen. / I don't think this will happen. / I hope this will happen!

E **Write one prediction for your life.**

In five years' time, I think I will ______________________

____

____

1 My job

Look at the photos. Complete with words from the box.

cashier ▪ customers ▪ friendly ▪ mechanic ▪ practical ▪ repair ▪ supermarket ▪ tools

Hi! I'm Sandra. I'm a ______________ . I ______________ cars. I like working with ______________ . I'm a ______________ person.

Hi! I'm Ahmad. I'm a ______________ . I work in a ______________ . I like working with ______________ . I'm very ______________ .

2 Applying for a job

Write the missing words.

details ▪ experience ▪ ~~form~~ ▪ interview ▪ job ▪ letter

1 application *form* ______________
2 contact ______________
3 cover ______________
4 job ______________
5 part-time ______________
6 work ______________

3 Where is it?

A Write the names of the office things.

file ▪ hole punch ▪ notepad ▪ scissors ▪ stapler

B Look at 3A. Circle the right answer.

1 The scissors are **on** / **next to** / **under** the notepad.
2 The stapler is **on** / **next to** / **under** the files.
3 The hole punch is **on** /**next to** / **under** the laptop.

4 Plans

Answer Bai's question.

I think I'll work out in the gym and meet my friend Marc next weekend.

And you? What do you think you'll do next weekend?

I think I'll ______________
______________ .

3 I can do it!

Game

How to play

coin

dice

1. Play in a small group.
2. Everyone needs one coin. The group needs a dice.
3. Put all the coins on 'START'.
4. **Player 1:** Throw the dice. Move your coin. Speak.
   Group: *Is the answer correct?*
   Yes = move forward (→) one box. /
   No = move back (←) 2 boxes.
5. **Player 2:** Throw the dice. Move your coin. Speak. ... Then **player 3** …
6. The **winner** of the game arrives at 'END' first.

START

1 Answer: How are you?	**2 Answer:** What is the weather like today? *The weather is … and …*	**3 Say** your name and spell it. *My name's … . That's: …*	**4 Name** two activities and where you do them. *You … in a …*
5 Ask about your friend's hobbies. *What … ?*	**6 Name** three ingredients in your favourite dish.	**7 Ask** about your friend's breakfast. *… you usually … for breakfast?*	**8 Say** the prices: a €0.20 b €12.50 c €99.99
9 Answer: When is your birthday? *My … . It's in …* (season).	**10 Say** the train times. a 08:00 b 11:30 c 15:22	**11 Answer:** What did you do yesterday? (two activities) *I … and …*	**12 Name** three jobs and places of work. *A … works in a …*
13 Answer: What are your job skills? (two skills) *I'm good at …*	**14 Name** three things in an office.	**15 Name** two of your strengths. *I'm … and …*	**16 Answer:** What will you do at the weekend? (two activities) *I'll … and …*

END

ingredients = *Zutaten*
strengths = *Stärken*

Unit 1, Part A, exercise 1

02 **Listen and fill in the gaps.**

1

Leah: Hi! How are you?

Linda: I'm ____________________ . And you?

Leah: I'm ________________ , too.

Linda: Nice __________________________ !

Leah: Nice to see you, too!

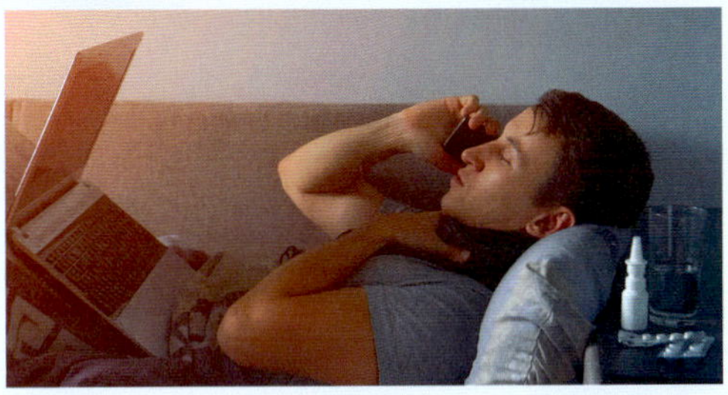

2

Manish: Hey! How are you?

Sam: I'm ____________________________ .

Manish: Are you OK?

Sam: No, ________________ . I'm sick.

3

Akin: Good morning! How are you?

Aisha: I'm ____________________ . How are you?

Akin: Oh, I'm OK, too.

Aisha: How is Auntie Jol?

Akin: She's fine. She's at a _______________ today.

Aisha: Really?

Unit 1, Part B, exercise 1

05 **Listen and complete the speech bubbles with words from the box.**

beat ▪ dancing ▪ pop music ▪ rap music

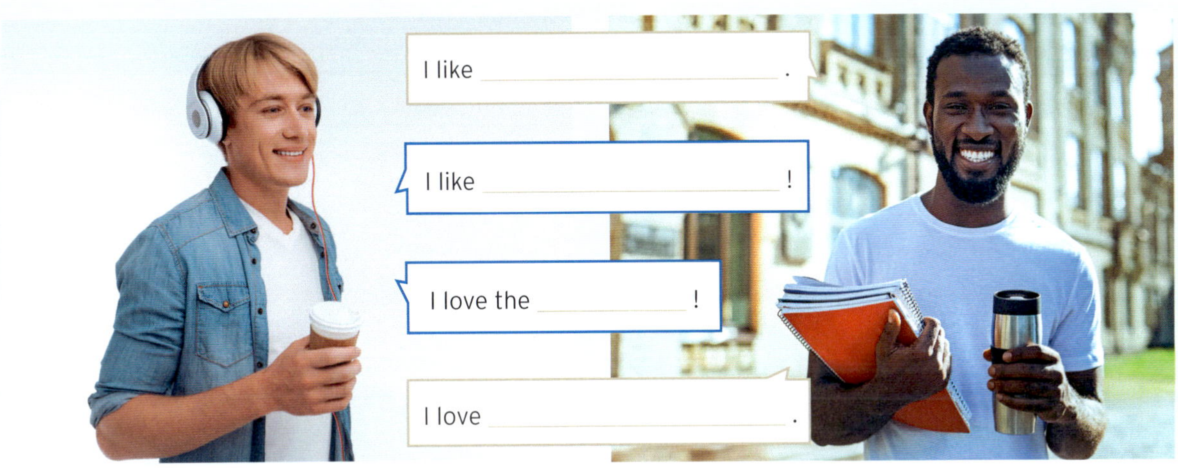

Unit 1, Part B, exercise 3B

07

Listen and complete.

Amira

Favourite pizza: ______________ *Favourite weather:* ______________

Favourite music: ______________ *Computer games are* ______________ *!*

Unit 1, Part B, exercise 4B

Complete the sentences.

The weather is ______________ . Amira and Farah go to the ______________ .

Olli and Tayo ______________ . Amira and Farah love the ______________ .

Amira loves pizza and Olli ______________ ______________ , too!

Unit 1, Part C, exercise 2A/B

09

A Listen and complete the questions.

1 What's your ______________ ?

2 And your ______________ ?

3 What's your ______________ ______________ ?

4 Do you have an ______________ ______________ ?

09

B Listen again and complete the form.

Name: Amira Ali

Address: ______ Green Road, London **Postcode:** E5 __ A __

Telephone number: __789__ 8614__

Email address: ______________@webnet.____

Unit 1, Part C, exercise 4

10

Listen and complete.

Café @ The Park

1 x ______________ with ______________

1 x ______________

= £ ______

Unit 2, Part A, exercise 1

13 **Listen and complete the speech bubbles with a word from the box. There are three extra words.**

best friend ▪ brother ▪ friendly ▪ football ▪ funny ▪ helpful ▪ nice ▪ video game

Marcus is my ______ ______. I can talk to him about my problems.

Janine is very nice and ______.

My friend Pablo is so ______!

Lamai is great! She's so ______.

Mesut is really cool. We're both ______ ______ fans.

Unit 2, Part A, exercise 3B

Match. There are two wrong answers.

1 Where does Amira live?
2 Who is Tayo?
3 Where's he from?
4 What's he like?
5 Why does Amira like him?

a Because he's kind and funny.
b He's from South Africa.
c He's very friendly.
d She lives in England.
e He's Amira's friend.
f He's from Nigeria.
g Because he's cool and creative.

Unit 2, Part B, exercise 3A

15 **Listen and complete.**

cooks / doesn't cook
plays / doesn't play
is/isn't
sings / doesn't sing
plays / doesn't play
speaks / doesn't speak

1 Olli ______ to his cousin Vicky.
2 Tayo ______ from Germany.
3 Tayo ______ the guitar.
4 Tayo ______ rock songs.
5 Nadima ______ Syrian food for Olli.
6 Olli ______ chess with Vicky.

Unit 2, Part B, exercise 5

Complete the sentences.

Amira and Olli want to go to the ____________ ____________ , but Farah doesn't want to do ____________ . She ____________ wants to do sport. Tayo is very happy. He thinks that ice cream is ____________ a good idea!

Unit 2, Part C, exercise 1A

16

Listen and complete.

1

football – park on ____________
at ________ p.m.

2

Great, thank you!

No problem. See you on ____________ at ____________ .

3

OK, see you on ____________ at ____________ at the café!

See you then!

Unit 2, Part C, exercise 2C/D

C Match the questions and answers.

a How can I help you?	1	b For which day, please?	
c For five people.		d And what time?	
e I'd like to book a table.	2	f It's Ali, Amira Ali.	
g For how many people?		h Seven p.m.	
i What's your name, please?		j Saturday, please.	

17

D Listen and put in the right order. Write numbers next to the speech bubbles.

Unit 3, Part A, exercise 3C

22 **Listen and complete.**

Katja:

Comes from: Germany

Lives in: ______

Misses: German ______

She doesn't eat ______ .

Yaa:

Comes from: Ghana

Lives in: ______

Misses: jollof ______

She eats it with fish and ______ .

Chris:

Comes from: ______

Lives in: Brazil

Misses: ______

Favourite dish: ______

curry with rice and Indian ______

Basam

Comes from: ______

Lives in: Canada

Misses: houmous, falafel and kebab with

mint ______

Iraqi food in Canada ______

______ the same.

Unit 3, Part B, exercise 1A/B

23 **A** **Listen and complete the shopping list.**

Food for the picnic

______ cake ______

______ and tomato ______ ______

______ salad ______

chips and ______ ______

a bottle of ______ ______

______ bottles of ______ ______

23 **B** **Who will bring what? Listen again and write: *A* = Amira, *T* = Tayo, *O* = Olli.**

Unit 3, Part C, exercise 1C

25 **Listen and write the price.**

1 €____.____ 2 £____.____ 3 $____.____ 4 AU$____

Unit 3, Part C, exercise 3A/B

A Read and complete.

Tayo: Let's buy some bread for the picnic.

Amira: Yes, good idea.

Tim: Hi! How ______________________ ?

Tayo: The baguettes look tasty.

Amira: Yes, how ______________________ are the baguettes?

Tim: One baguette is one pound ten pence.

Amira: I'______________________ three baguettes.

Tim: Three? OK, That's three pounds thirty.

Amira: Sorry. Could ______________________ ?

Tim: Three pounds thirty pence, please.

Amira: Here you are.

Tim: Thank you. Have ______________________ !

Amira: You, too! Bye!

B Listen and check. 26

Unit 4, Part A, exercise 2C

Listen and complete. There are two extra words. 30

December ▪ fireworks ▪ hats ▪ January ▪ party ▪ T-shirts ▪ winter

My favourite festival is in __________ , on the 31st of ______________ . It's New Year's Eve. We say 'bye' to the old year and 'hello' to the new year! I usually have a __________ with my friends. We wear funny __________ ! We eat tasty food, then we listen to music and dance! At midnight, we go and watch the ______________ in the street.

Unit 4, Part B, exercise 2A/B

31

A **Listen and put the sentences in order (1–7).**

____ They ate Irish stew for lunch.
____ They bought a coffee.
____ They visited Dublin Castle.
____ They did a boat trip.
____ They went shopping.
____ They watched TV.
____ They walked next to the river.

River Liffey

Dublin Castle

Irish stew

B **Work with a partner. Check your answers.**

Unit 4, Part C, exercise 3

32

Listen and complete.

Booking form

Number of people: ____________ Number of nights: ____________
Number of rooms: ____________ Name: *Rahul* ____________
Dates: ______ – ______ *of June* Phone number: ____________

Unit 4, Part C, exercise 5A/B

34

A **Listen and write the missing information.**

Train departures

Time	Destination	Platform
11:45	Oxford	____
____:02	London Paddington	5
13:23	Watford	____
14:____	Manchester	13
14:43	Liverpool	____
15:____	Birmingham	7

B **Now check your answers with a partner. Read your answers out loud.**

Unit 5, Part A, exercise 3A

36 **Read, listen and find the words.**

I don't like working with *c*__________*s* and I'm not so good at organizing things, so I don't want an *o*__________ job. I'm good at working with my hands, so I want to do something practical. I'd like to work with *t*__________ and make things!

I don't like cold weather, so I don't want to work outside! I'm not good at selling things or working with *m*__________. I'd like to work independently, but with nice *c*__________ and of course a nice boss! I'm good at *o*__________ things and working on the computer, so I'd like an office job.

I'm good at looking after people and helping them to feel *g*__________. I'm not very good at working with my hands, so I wouldn't want to be a painter or a *m*__________ worker. I'd like to work with older *p*__________ because they can tell me interesting stories about their lives.

Unit 5, Part B, exercise 3A/B

39 **A Look at the photos and listen. Complete the speech bubbles.**

1 Excuse __________, __________ reception, please?

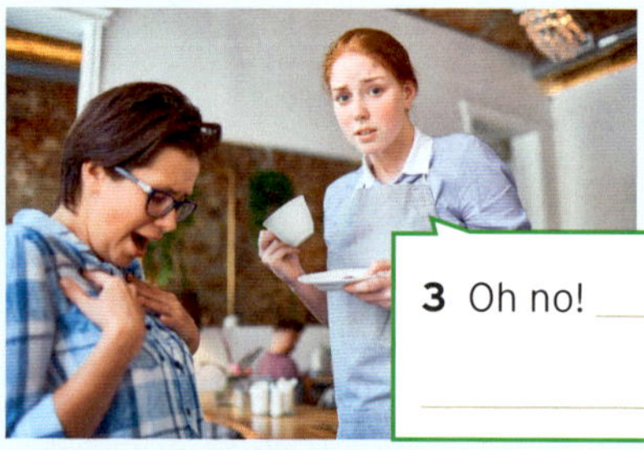

3 Oh no! __________ __________!

2 Excuse me, what's __________ __________, please?

4 Good morning. I'm Tim. __________ I'm __________!

39

B Listen again and complete the sentences.

1 The ______________ is straight on and on the ______________ .

2 The time is ______________ .

3 The customer had a new ______________ .

4 The waitress offered her a free ______________ .

5 Tim was late because he missed the ______________ .

Unit 6, Part A, exercise 1A

43

Listen and write the missing word.

1 Tayo is happy because he'll start ______________ soon.

2 He'll work in ______________ .

3 After the apprenticeship, Tayo will be a ______________ .

4 He'll start his apprenticeship next ______________ .

5 Amira will ______________ in the summer.

Tell me more about your apprenticeship, Tayo.

Unit 6, Part B, exercise 1A

Complete Tayo's questions with a word from the box. Use the words only one time.

company ■ How ■ months ■ tasks ■ Where

1 What's the name of the ______________ ?

2 ______________ is the internship?

3 For how many ______________ is the internship?

4 Which ______________ will the intern do?

5 ______________ do you apply for the internship?

I don't know which internship to apply for! I think I'll ask Tayo for help!

44

Now listen to Tayo's questions and check your answers.

Video tasks

1 Everyday English

1

A Write the correct letter (a–e).

a Can you help me, please? **b** Happy birthday!
c Sorry! **d** Congratulations! **e** Bye! See you soon!

1

Oh, ____________ !

2

____________ !

3

They're there.

____________ ?
Where are the pizzas?

4

Here you are.
____________ !

5

You're the winner!
____________ !

B Circle the correct option.

Give me / I'd like / I want
a ticket for the movie, please.

Please! / Welcome! / You're welcome!

Thank. / Thanks you. / Thank you.

2 The Notting Hill Carnival

2

A Circle the right answer.

1 Notting Hill is in the west of **England / London / the Caribbean**.

2 In Notting Hill, many people have family from **Africa / the Caribbean / the USA.**

3 The Notting Hill Carnival is in **August / February / June.**

4 **Lots of / No / Not many** people visit the Notting Hill Carnival.

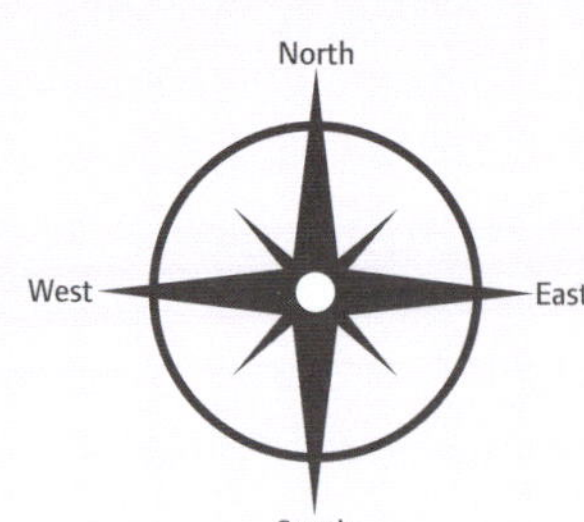

B Tick (✔) four right options.

- [ ] dance
- [ ] listen to music
- [ ] do a boat trip
- [ ] see colourful costumes
- [ ] eat and drink
- [ ] sing songs
- [ ] go shopping
- [ ] watch a show

C Circle the right photo.

1 Which is a typical instrument from the Caribbean?

an electric guitar

a steel drum

a trumpet

2 Which is a typical Caribbean dish?

falafel

fish and chips

pepperpot stew

D Complete with the right words.

bread ▪ fish ▪ pineapple ▪ spicy

1 Jerk chicken is ______________________ .

2 Roti is a kind of ______________________ .

3 You can eat a patty with vegetables, meat or ______________________ .

4 You can drink fresh ______________________ juice at the Carnival.

E **Now you** Talk. Answer Ben's questions.

3 Booking in English

3

A Find the words.

1 A one way ticket: (NISELG) ________

2 To travel to a place and come back, you need a (TRERNU) ________ ticket.

3 A different word for 'book'; e.g. I'd like to (SREREEV) ________ a seat.

4 A different word for 'leaves'; e.g. the train (EPDRAST) ________ at 17:35.

5 Would you like a table seat or a (NWIOWD) ________ seat?

B Circle the right options.

They want to come to London and go back to Birmingham.

1 **Two / Three** clients will come to London.

2 The clients want **return / single** train ticket.

3 The clients will travel from **Birmingham / London**.

4 They will arrive at **10 a.m. / 10 p.m.** and leave at **5 a.m. / 5 p.m.**

5 Your boss **wants / doesn't want** you to book accommodation in London.

C Complete.

Hotel Victoria. David speaking. How can I ________ ________ ?

Good afternoon. This is Chiara Santini from We-Tech.

1

2 **David:** Would you like two ________ rooms or a ________ room?
Chiara: ________ , please.

3 **David:** With or without ________ ?
Chiara: ________ , please.

4 **David:** Can I take your name and ________ ________ please?
Chiara: Yes, it's Chiara Santini.
David: Sorry? Can you ________ your ________ name, please?

5 **Chiara:** And the number is: 02 __ 57 __ 926 __ 4.

A

a.m. [ˌeɪ ˈem] 15 *(Uhrzeit:)* vormittags
a, an [ə, ən] 4 ein/e
about [əˈbaʊt] 4 über; 33 ungefähr
activity [ækˈtɪvəti] 14 Tätigkeit, Beschäftigung, Aktivität
ad(vert) [ˈæd(vɜːt)] 54 Anzeige
to add sth [æd] 28 etw hinzufügen
address [əˈdres] 8 Adresse
administration [ədˌmɪnɪˈstreɪʃn] 53 Verwaltung, Direktion
administrative [ədˈmɪnɪstrətɪv] 55 Verwaltungs-
adult [ˈædʌlt] 37 Erwachsene/r
advert [ˈædvɜːt] 57 Anzeige
after [ˈɑːftə] 14 nach
afternoon [ˌɑːftəˈnuːn] 8 Nachmittag
in the afternoon [ɪn ði ˌɑːftəˈnuːn] 11 am Nachmittag
again [əˈgen] 24 noch einmal
air [eə] 28 Luft
alarm clock [əˈlɑːm klɒk] 45 Wecker
all [ɔːl] 12 alle
all day [ɔːl ˈdeɪ] 11 den ganzen Tag lang
all the time [ˌɔːl ðə ˈtaɪm] 23 ständig, andauernd
all year round [ˌɔːl jɪə ˈraʊnd] 30 das ganze Jahr (über)
already [ɔːlˈredi] 52 schon
also [ˈɔːlsəʊ] 29 auch
always [ˈɔːlweɪz] 12 immer, ständig
and [ənd] 3 und
angry: to get angry [ˌget ˈæŋgri] 56 sich ärgern, sich aufregen
animal [ˈænɪml] 6 Tier
another [əˈnʌðə] 46 noch ein/e
answer [ˈɑːnsə] 12 Antwort
to answer sth [ˈɑːnsə] 19 etw beantworten
anything [ˈeniθɪŋ] 26 etwas
anyway [ˈeniweɪ] 12 sowieso, jedenfalls
apartment [əˈpɑːtmənt] 38 Wohnung
apple [ˈæpl] 25 Apfel
application [ˌæplɪˈkeɪʃn] 57 Bewerbung
to apply for a job [əˌplaɪ fər ə ˈdʒɒb] 54 sich auf eine Stelle bewerben
appointment [əˈpɔɪntmənt] 58 Termin
to make an appointment [ˌmeɪk ən əˈpɔɪntmənt] 58 einen Termin vereinbaren
apprentice [əˈprentɪs] 51 Auszubildende/r, Lehrling
apprenticeship [əˈprentɪʃɪp] 51 Lehrstelle, Ausbildung
April [ˈeɪprəl] 30 April
area [ˈeəriə] 35 Bereich
around [əˈraʊnd] 30 um … herum
around the world [əˌraʊnd ðə ˈwɜːld] 26 weltweit, auf der ganzen Welt
to arrive [əˈraɪv] 37 eintreffen, ankommen
to ask [ɑːsk] 24 fragen
to ask for sth [ˈɑːsk fə] 46 um etw bitten
to ask sb a question [ˌɑːsk ə ˈkwestʃən] 41 jdm eine Frage stellen
to assist with sth [əˈsɪst wɪð] 53 bei etw assistieren
at [æt] 4 bei, auf; 8 an, in; 16 *(Uhrzeit:)* um
atmosphere [ˈætməsfɪə] 35 Atmosphäre
to attach sth [əˈtætʃ] 57 *(E-Mail:)* etw anhängen
attraction [əˈtrækʃn] 38 Attraktion
aubergine [ˈəʊbəʒiːn] 21 Aubergine
August [ˈɔːgəst] 30 August
auntie [ˈɑːnti] 4 Tante
autumn [ˈɔːtəm] 30 Herbst
away [əˈweɪ] 35 weg

B

back [bæk] 62 zurück
bad [bæd] 43 schlecht, schlimm
bag [bæg] 48 Tasche
to bake [beɪk] 24 backen, braten
baker [ˈbeɪkə] 53 Bäcker/in
bakery [ˈbeɪkəri] 25 Bäckerei
banana [bəˈnɑːnə] 23 Banane
barbecue [ˈbɑːbɪkjuː] 30 Grillfest
basic knowledge [ˌbeɪsɪk ˈnɒlɪdʒ] 58 Grundkenntnisse
bathroom [ˈbɑːθruːm] 34 Badezimmer, Bad
to be [bi] 3 sein
to be right [bi ˈraɪt] 15 recht haben
to be wrong [bi ˈrɒŋ] 15 unrecht haben, sich irren
beach [biːtʃ] 31 Strand
beautiful [ˈbjuːtɪfl] 33 schön
because [bɪˈkɒz] 13 weil
bed [bed] 35 Bett
beef [biːf] 21 Rindfleisch
before [bɪˈfɔː] 15 vor
best [best] 6 beste/r/s
big [bɪg] 18 groß
bike [baɪk] 36 Fahrrad
birthday [ˈbɜːθdeɪ] 16 Geburtstag
bit: a bit [ə ˈbɪt] 5 ein bisschen
blouse [blaʊz] 46 Bluse
blue [bluː] 30 blau
board [bɔːd] 48 Tafel
boat [bəʊt] 33 Boot
boat trip [ˈbəʊt trɪp] 33 Bootsfahrt
body [ˈbɒdi] 56 Körper
to boil sth [bɔɪl] 28 etw (in Wasser) kochen
bonfire [ˈbɒnfaɪə] 30 (großes) Feuer, Freudenfeuer
book [bʊk] 48 Buch
to book [bʊk] 16 reservieren, buchen
booked [bʊkt] 17 reserviert, gebucht
booking [ˈbʊkɪŋ] 17 Reservierung, Buchung
boring [ˈbɔːrɪŋ] 7 langweilig
boss [bɒs] 43 Chef/in
both [bəʊθ] 12 beide
bottle [ˈbɒtl] 24 Flasche
bottom [ˈbɒtəm] 48 unterste/r/s
box [bɒks] 12 Kasten, Kästchen; 48 Schachtel, Kiste
boyfriend [ˈbɔɪfrend] 12 Freund
bread [bred] 21 Brot
breakfast [ˈbrekfəst] 33 Frühstück
to bring sth [brɪŋ] 24 etw mitbringen; 60 etw bringen
brother [ˈbrʌðə] 12 Bruder
brown [braʊn] 33 braun
budget [ˈbʌdʒɪt] 38 Budget, finanzieller Rahmen
bunk bed [ˈbʌnk bed] 35 Etagenbett
bus [bʌs] 33 Bus
bus stop [ˈbʌs stɒp] 45 Bushaltestelle
busy [ˈbɪzi] 53 geschäftig, belebt, gut ausgelastet
to be busy [bi ˈbɪzi] 16 (viel) zu tun haben, beschäftigt sein
but [bʌt] 14 aber
butter [ˈbʌtə] 21 Butter
to buy [baɪ] 16 kaufen
by bus [baɪ ˈbʌs] 35 mit dem Bus
by car [baɪ ˈkɑː] 35 mit dem Auto
by the lake [baɪ ðə ˈleɪk] 35 am See
Bye. [baɪ] 8 Auf Wiedersehen! 17 Tschüss!

C

café [ˈkæfeɪ] 7 Café
cake [keɪk] 9 Kuchen
to call sth sth [kɔːl] 38 etw etw nennen
camera [ˈkæmərə] 60 Kamera
camp [kæmp] 35 Zeltlager
campsite [ˈkæmpsaɪt] 35 Campingplatz
can [kæn] 8 können; 28 Dose
candle [ˈkændl] 30 Kerze
capital city [ˌkæpɪtl ˈsɪti] 53 Hauptstadt
car [kɑː] 20 Auto
car repair shop [ˈkɑː rɪpeə ʃɒp] 41 Autowerkstatt
card [kɑːd] 50 Karte
care home [ˈkeə həʊm] 41 Pflegeheim
carer [ˈkeərə] 41 Pfleger/in, Betreuer/in

iː	ɪ	e	æ	ɑː	ɒ	ɔː	ʊ	uː	ʌ	ɜː	ə	i	u
see	in	yes	apple	car	got	or	put	too	cut	girl	sister	happy	you

caring [ˈkeərɪŋ] 53 fürsorglich, liebevoll
carnival [ˈkɑːnɪvl] 30 Karneval
carpenter [ˈkɑːpəntə] 56 Schreiner/in, Tischler/in
carrot [ˈkærət] 28 Möhre, Karotte
cashier [kæˈʃɪə] 41 Kassierer/in
castle [ˈkɑːsl] 33 Burg, Schloss
cat [kæt] 10 Katze
to catch sth [kætʃ] 28 etw auffangen
cauliflower [ˈkɒliflaʊə] 28 Blumenkohl
caviar [ˈkæviɑː] 29 Kaviar
to celebrate [ˈselɪbreɪt] 29 feiern
cent [sent] 26 Cent
centre [ˈsentə] 32 Zentrum, Mitte
chair [tʃeə] 48 Stuhl
to change sth [tʃeɪndʒ] 17 etw ändern
chat [tʃæt] 13 Chat *(im Internet)*
to chat to/with sb [ˈtʃæt tə/wɪð] 14 mit jdm sprechen, sich mit jdm unterhalten, mit jdm plaudern
cheap [tʃiːp] 26 billig, günstig
to check sth [tʃek] 15 etw überprüfen
checkout [ˈtʃekaʊt] 25 Kasse
cheese [tʃiːz] 21 Käse
chess [tʃes] 14 Schach
chicken [ˈtʃɪkɪn] 21 Huhn, Hühnchen
child, children [tʃaɪld, ˈtʃɪldrən] 37 Kind, Kinder
childcare [ˈtʃaɪldkeə] 53 Kinderbetreuung
chilli [ˈtʃɪli] 23 Chili
chips *pl* [tʃɪps] 22 Pommes frites
chocolate [ˈtʃɒklət] 9 Schokolade
choice [tʃɔɪs] 29 Auswahl
to choose [tʃuːz] 12 auswählen, aussuchen
Christmas [ˈkrɪsməs] 30 Weihnachten
cinema [ˈsɪnəmə] 14 Kino
to circle sth [ˈsɜːkl] 3 etw umkringeln
circus [ˈsɜːkəs] 42 Zirkus
city [ˈsɪti] 53 Stadt, Großstadt
class [klɑːs] 10 Klasse, Kurs
classmate [ˈklɑːsmeɪt] 12 Klassenkamerad/in
classroom [ˈklɑːsruːm] 48 Klassenzimmer
clean [kliːn] 38 sauber
cleaner [ˈkliːnə] 41 Reinigungskraft
clever [ˈklevə] 12 klug, intelligent
client [ˈklaɪənt] 58 Kunde/Kundin
clock: … o'clock [əˈklɒk] 44 … Uhr
close to sb/sth [ˈkləʊs tə] 35 nahe an/bei jdm/etw
closed [kləʊzd] 17 geschlossen
clothes *pl* [kləʊðz] 15 Kleider, Kleidung, Klamotten
cloud [klaʊd] 56 Wolke
cloudy [ˈklaʊdi] 5 bewölkt, bedeckt
coffee [ˈkɒfi] 9 Kaffee
to go for a coffee [ˌgəʊ fər ə ˈkɒfi] 16 einen Kaffee trinken gehen
coin [kɔɪn] 26 Münze
cold [kəʊld] 5 kalt
colleague [ˈkɒliːg] 43 Kollege/Kollegin
colour [ˈkʌlə] 30 Farbe
colourful [ˈkʌləfl] 30 bunt, farbenfroh
to come in [ˌkʌm ˈɪn] 20 hereinkommen, eintreten
comfortable [ˈkʌmftəbl] 35 behaglich, gemütlich, komfortabel
to communicate [kəˈmjuːnɪkeɪt] 53 kommunizieren
communicative [kəˈmjuːnɪkətɪv] 55 kommunikativ, aufgeschlossen
company [ˈkʌmpəni] 45 Unternehmen, Firma
to complete sth [kəmˈpliːt] 5 etw vervollständigen, etw ausfüllen
concert [ˈkɒnsət] 14 Konzert
to confirm sth [kənˈfɜːm] 17 etw bestätigen
Congratulations! [kənˌgrætʃʊˈleɪʃnz] 51 Herzlichen Glückwunsch!
consonant [ˈkɒnsənənt] 41 Konsonant
construction [kənˈstrʌkʃn] 53 Bau, Baugewerbe
construction site [kənˈstrʌkʃn saɪt] 43 Baustelle
construction worker [kənˈstrʌkʃn wɜːkə] 53 Bauarbeiter/in
to contact sb [ˈkɒntækt] 57 sich an jdn wenden, sich mit jdm in Verbindung setzen
contact (person) [ˈkɒntækt] 57 Ansprechpartner/in
contact details *pl* [ˈkɒntækt diːteɪlz] 58 Kontaktdaten
to cook [kʊk] 3 kochen, zubereiten
cook [kʊk] 41 Koch/Köchin
cookie [ˈkʊki] 21 Keks
cooking [ˈkʊkɪŋ] 15 Kochen
cool [kuːl] 12 cool
corner [ˈkɔːnə] 47 Ecke
correct [kəˈrekt] 20 richtig, korrekt
to correct sth [kəˈrekt] 46 etw berichtigen, etw korrigieren
correspondence [ˌkɒrɪˈspɒndəns] 58 Korrespondenz, Schriftverkehr
to cost [kɒst] 38 kosten
costume [ˈkɒstjuːm] 30 Kostüm
to count [kaʊnt] 11 zählen
country [ˈkʌntri] 4 Land
home country [ˌhəʊm ˈkʌntri] 23 Heimatland
countryside [ˈkʌntrisaɪd] 35 Land
course: of course [əf ˈkɔːs] 12 natürlich, selbstverständlich
cousin [ˈkʌzn] 13 Cousin/Cousine
crazy [ˈkreɪzi] 5 verrückt
You are crazy! [juː ˌɑː ˈkreɪzi] 5 Du spinnst!
cream [kriːm] 21 Sahne
to create sth [kriˈeɪt] 29 etw gestalten, etw machen
creative [kriˈeɪtɪv] 13 kreativ
cucumber [ˈkjuːkʌmbə] 21 Gurke
culture [ˈkʌltʃə] 30 Kultur
cup [kʌp] 11 Tasse
cup of tea [kʌp əf ˈtiː] 11 Tasse Tee
cupboard [ˈkʌbəd] 47 Schrank
customer [ˈkʌstəmə] 17 Kunde/Kundin
to cut [kʌt] 28 schneiden
CV *BE* [ˌsiː ˈviː] 55 Lebenslauf

D

dairy (products) [ˈdeəri] 21 Milchprodukte
to dance [dɑːns] 3 tanzen
date [deɪt] 36 Datum
day [deɪ] 5 Tag
all day [ɔːl ˈdeɪ] 11 den ganzen Tag lang
Dear Sir or Madam [dɪə ˌsɜːr ɔː ˈmædəm] 57 Sehr geehrte Damen und Herren
December [dɪˈsembə] 30 Dezember
to decide [dɪˈsaɪd] 54 sich entscheiden
decoration [ˌdekəˈreɪʃn] 30 Dekoration, Schmuck
delicious [dɪˈlɪʃəs] 23 delikat, schmackhaft, lecker
to depart [dɪˈpɑːt] 36 abfahren
departure [dɪˈpɑːtʃə] 36 Abfahrt
to describe [dɪˈskraɪb] 20 beschreiben
desk [desk] 47 Schreibtisch
dessert [dɪˈzɜːt] 25 Nachtisch
destination [ˌdestɪˈneɪʃn] 36 Ziel
details *pl*: **contact details** *pl* [ˈkɒntækt diːteɪlz] 58 Kontakdaten
dice [daɪs] 62 Würfel
diet [ˈdaɪət] 21 Ernährung, Nahrung, Kost
different [ˈdɪfrənt] 14 verschieden
dinner [ˈdɪnə] 16 Abendessen
dish [dɪʃ] 22 Gericht, Speise
district [ˈdɪstrɪkt] 34 Gebiet
to do [duː] 6 tun, machen
to do a task [ˌduː ə ˈtɑːsk] 53 eine Aufgabe erledigen
to do sport [du ˈspɔːt] 11 Sport treiben
document [ˈdɒkjumənt] 34 Dokument

tʃ	dʒ	ʃ	ʒ	θ	ð	ŋ	s	z	v	w
chip	jet	ship	garage	thing	the	ring	ice	as	very	wet

dog [dɒg] 10 Hund
dot [dɒt] 8 Punkt
double room [ˌdʌbl ˈru:m] 34 Doppelzimmer
to draw [drɔ:] 49 zeichnen
dream [dri:m] 52 Traum
to drink [drɪŋk] 11 trinken
drink [drɪŋk] 24 Getränk
to drive [draɪv] 41 fahren
driver [ˈdraɪvə] 41 Fahrer/in
to dry [draɪ] 42 trocknen
during [ˈdjʊərɪŋ] 38 während

E

e.g. [ˌi: ˈdʒi:] 57 z.B.
each [i:tʃ] 25 jede/r/s (einzelne)
to earn money [ɜ:n ˈmʌni] 46 Geld verdienen
to eat [i:t] 11 essen
education [ˌedʒuˈkeɪʃn] 59 Schulbildung, Bildung, Ausbildung
egg [eg] 21 Ei
Eid [i:d] 31 Fastenbrechen, Zuckerfest
else: Anything else? [ˌeniθɪŋ ˈels] 26 Sonst noch etwas?
email [ˈi:meɪl] 8 E-Mail
employment [ɪmˈplɔɪmənt] 53 Beschäftigung, Anstellung
empty [ˈempti] 49 leer
to enclose sth [ɪnˈkləʊz] 57 *(Brief:)* etw beifügen
end [end] 30 Ende
energy [ˈenədʒi] 56 Energie
engine [ˈendʒɪn] 42 Motor
English-speaking [ˈɪŋglɪʃ spi:kɪŋ] 30 englischsprachig
to enjoy sth [ɪnˈdʒɔɪ] 26 etw genießen
to enjoy doing sth [ɪnˈdʒɔɪ] 55 etw gern tun
enthusiastic [ɪnˌθju:ziˈæstɪk] 56 begeisterungsfähig
equipment [ɪˈkwɪpmənt] 53 Geräte, Ausstattung
euro [ˈjʊərəʊ] 26 Euro
evening [ˈi:vnɪŋ] 11 Abend
in the evening [ɪn ði ˈi:vnɪŋ] 11 am Abend
every [ˈevri] 7 jede/r/s
everybody [ˈevribɒdi] 12 jeder, jedem, jeden
everyone [ˈevriwʌn] 12 jeder, jedem, jeden
everyone [ˈevriwʌn] 31 jeder, alle
everything [ˈevriθɪŋ] 38 alles
everywhere [ˈevriweə] 30 überall
exactly [ɪgˈzæktli] 23 genau
exactly the same [ɪgˌzæktli ðə ˈseɪm] 23 genauso, genau gleich
excellent [ˈeksələnt] 58 ausgezeichnet, hervorragend
excited: to be excited about sth [bi ɪkˈsaɪtɪd əbaʊt] 56 von etw begeistert sein
exciting [ɪkˈsaɪtɪŋ] 38 aufregend, spannend
to excuse [ɪkˈskju:z] 25 entschuldigen
Excuse me! [ɪkˈskju:z mi:] 25 Entschuldigung! Verzeihung!
expensive [ɪkˈspensɪv] 35 teuer
experience [ɪkˈspɪəriəns] 51 Erfahrung; 55 Erlebnis(se)
to get/gain experience [ˌget/ˌgeɪn ɪkˈspɪəriəns] 51 Erfahrung(en) sammeln
experiment [ɪkˈsperɪmənt] 53 Versuch, Experiment
extra [ˈekstrə] 12 zusätzlich, zu viel
eye [aɪ] 38 Auge

F

face [feɪs] 30 Gesicht
factory [ˈfæktəri] 41 Fabrik
fair [feə] 12 gerecht, fair
false [fɔ:ls] 15 falsch, unzutreffend
famous [ˈfeɪməs] 60 berühmt
fan [fæn] 12 Fan
fashion [ˈfæʃn] 53 Mode
fast [fɑ:st] 45 schnell
fat [fæt] 21 Fett
favourite [ˈfeɪvərɪt] 5 Lieblings-
February [ˈfebruəri] 30 Februar
to feel [fi:l] 12 fühlen, sich fühlen
festival [ˈfestɪvl] 30 Fest, Festtag, Feiertag
file [faɪl] 48 Mappe, (Akten-)Ordner
to file sth [faɪl] 42 etw *(Dokumente usw.)* ablegen, etw abheften
to fill sth in [ˌfɪl ˈɪn] 4 etw ausfüllen
filling [ˈfɪlɪŋ] 29 Füllung
to find [faɪnd] 13 finden
to find out sth [ˌfaɪnd ˈaʊt] 48 etw herausfinden
fine [faɪn] 4 gut, in Ordnung, ausgezeichnet
I'm fine. [aɪm ˈfaɪn] 4 Mir geht es gut.
That's fine. [ðəts ˈfaɪn] 16 Das ist in Ordnung.
to finish [ˈfɪnɪʃ] 16 zu Ende sein
fireworks *pl* [ˈfaɪəwɜ:ks] 30 Feuerwerk
fish [fɪʃ] 21 Fisch
fit [fɪt] 53 in Form, fit
flag [flæg] 30 Flagge
flat *BE* [flæt] 60 Wohnung
flexible [ˈfleksəbl] 56 flexibel
flour [ˈflaʊə] 24 Mehl
flyer [ˈflaɪə] 26 Prospekt, Reklamezettel
food [fu:d] 11 Essen, Speisen, Lebensmittel
football [ˈfʊtbɔ:l] 3 Fußball
footballer [ˈfʊtbɔ:lə] 60 Fußballer/in
for [ˌef əʊ ˈɑ:] 8 für
for one hour [fə ˌwʌn ˈhaʊə] 15 eine Stunde (lang)
for breakfast [fə ˈbrekfəst] 33 zum Frühstück
to forget [fəˈget] 25 vergessen
form [fɔ:m] 8 Formular
forward [ˈfɔ:wəd] 62 vorwärts
free [fri:] 6 frei; 26 kostenlos, gratis
for free [fə ˈfri:] 46 umsonst
free time [ˌfri: ˈtaɪm] 6 Freizeit
fresh [freʃ] 23 frisch
Friday [ˈfraɪdeɪ] 16 Freitag
on Fridays [ɒn ˈfraɪdeɪz] 37 freitags
friend [frend] 7 Freund/in
to make friends [meɪk ˈfrendz] 35 Freunde finden, Freundschaften schließen
from [frəm] 3 aus
where ... from [ˌweə ˈfrɒm] 13 woher
from the top [frəm ðə ˈtɒp] 38 von oben
frozen foods *pl* [ˌfrəʊzn ˈfu:d] 25 Tiefkühlkost
fruit [fru:t] 21 Obst, Frucht, Früchte
to fry [fraɪ] 28 etw (in der Pfanne) braten
frying pan [ˈfraɪɪŋ pæn] 28 Bratpfanne
full [fʊl] 17 voll
full-time [ˌfʊl ˈtaɪm] 44 Vollzeit-
fun [fʌn] 32 Spaß
to be fun [bi ˈfʌn] 32 Spaß machen
to join in the fun [dʒɔɪn ˌɪn ðə ˈfʌn] 32 mitmachen
funny [ˈfʌni] 12 lustig
future [ˈfju:tʃə] 51 Zukunft; 53 zukünftig

G

to gain experience [ˌgeɪn ɪkˈspɪəriəns] 53 Erfahrung(en) sammeln
game [geɪm] 7 Spiel
gap [gæp] 4 Lücke
garden [ˈgɑ:dn] 30 Garten
garlic [ˈgɑ:lɪk] 21 Knoblauch
to get angry [ˌget ˈæŋgri] 56 sich ärgern, sich aufregen
to get sth [get] 25 etw holen; 26 etw bekommen; 51 sich etw besorgen
to get somewhere [ˈget sʌmweə] 36 wohin gelangen, wohin kommen
to get up [ˌget ˈʌp] 15 aufstehen
to go [gəʊ] 7 gehen
to go out [ˌgəʊ ˈaʊt] 16 ausgehen

i:	ɪ	e	æ	ɑ:	ɒ	ɔ:	ʊ	u:	ʌ	ɜ:	ə	i	u
see	in	yes	apple	car	got	or	put	too	cut	girl	sister	happy	you

Go away! [ˌɡəʊ əˈweɪ] 27 Hau ab!
good [ɡʊd] 4 gut;
I'm not so good. [ˌaɪm ˈnɒt səʊ ɡʊd] 4 Mir geht es nicht so gut.
to be good at doing sth [bi ˈɡʊd ət] 43 etw gut können
Good luck! [ˌɡʊd ˈlʌk] 51 Viel Glück!
goodbye [ˌɡʊdˈbaɪ] 17 auf Wiedersehen
grains *pl* [ɡreɪnz] 21 Getreide
grandma [ˈɡrænmɑː] 13 Oma
grape [ɡreɪp] 21 Traube
great [ɡreɪt] 12 großartig, toll
green [ɡriːn] 8 grün
group [ɡruːp] 11 Gruppe
to guess [ɡes] 3 raten, erraten
guest [ɡest] 52 Gast
guitar [ɡɪˈtɑː] 14 Gitarre
to play the guitar [ˌpleɪ ðə ɡɪˈtɑː] 14 Gitarre spielen
guys *pl* [ɡaɪz] 12 Leute
gym [dʒɪm] 61 Fitness-Studio

H

hair [heə] 42 Haar(e)
hairdresser [ˈheədresə] 42 Friseur/in
half [hɑːf] 26 halb
hand [hænd] 29 Hand
to hang out with sb [ˌhæŋ ˈaʊt wɪð] 11 mit jdm abhängen, sich mit jdm treffen
Hanukka [ˈhʌnʊkə] 31 Chanukka, Lichterfest
to happen [ˈhæpən] 60 geschehen
happy [ˈhæpi] 12 glücklich, zufrieden, fröhlich
to be happy to do sth [bi ˈhæpi tə duː] 35 etw gern tun; gern bereit sein, etw zu tun
hard [hɑːd] 52 schwer, hart
hard-working [ˌhɑːd ˈwɜːkɪŋ] 55 fleißig
hat [hæt] 30 Mütze, Hut
to hate [heɪt] 5 gar nicht mögen, hassen
to have [hæv] 8 haben
to have a look [həv ə ˈlʊk] 27 sich etw ansehen
he [hiː] 12 er
health [helθ] 4 Gesundheit
healthy [ˈhelθi] 21 gesund
to hear [hɪə] 27 hören
hello [həˈləʊ] 14 hallo
to say hello to sb [ˌseɪ həˈləʊ tə] 38 jdn begrüßen, jdm guten Tag sagen
to help [help] 8 helfen
helpful [ˈhelpfl] 12 hilfsbereit
her [hɜː] 13 ihr
here [hɪə] 9 hier
just here [ˌdʒʌst ˈhɪə] 25 genau hier
Here you are! [ˌhɪə ju ˈɑː] 9 *(Übergabe:)* Bitte sehr! Bitteschön!
Here you go! [ˌhɪə ju ˈɡəʊ] 26 *(Übergabe:)* Bitte sehr! Bitteschön!
him [hɪm] 13 ihm, ihn
his [hɪz] 12 sein/e
hole punch [ˈhəʊl pʌntʃ] 48 Locher
holiday [ˈhɒlədeɪ] 35 Urlaub, Ferien
on holiday [ɒn ˈhɒlədeɪ] 35 im Urlaub
to go on holiday [ɡəʊ ɒn ˈhɒlədeɪ] 51 in Urlaub fahren, Urlaub machen
home [həʊm] 23 Heimat; 38 Zuhause
at home [ət ˈhəʊm] 11 zu Hause
home country [ˌhəʊm ˈkʌntri] 23 Heimatland
home-cooked [ˌhəʊm ˈkʊkt] 35 selbst zubereitet
homemade [ˌhəʊmˈmeɪd] 35 selbstgemacht
honey [ˈhʌni] 29 Honig
to hope [həʊp] 29 hoffen
hostel [ˈhɒstl] 35 Herberge, Hostel
hot [hɒt] 5 heiß
hotel [həʊˈtel] 34 Hotel
houmous [ˈhʊməs] 23 Hummus
hour [ˈaʊə] 15 Stunde
for one hour [fə ˌwʌn ˈhaʊə] 15 eine Stunde (lang)
house [haʊs] 33 Haus
how [haʊ] 4 wie; 12 auf welche Weise, inwiefern
How are you? [ˌhaʊ ə ˈjuː] 4 Wie geht es Ihnen/dir?
how many? [haʊ ˈmeni] 11 wie viel(e)?
how much? [haʊ ˈmʌtʃ] 25 wie viel?
How much is/are …? [haʊ ˈmʌtʃ ɪz/ɑː] 26 Wie viel kostet/kosten …?
hungry [ˈhʌŋɡri] 21 hungrig
to be hungry [bi ˈhʌŋɡri] 21 Hunger haben
hygiene [ˈhaɪdʒiːn] 53 Hygiene

I

I [aɪ] 3 ich
ice cream [ˌaɪs ˈkriːm] 15 Eis, Eiskrem
idea [aɪˈdɪə] 10 Idee, Einfall, Gedanke
ideal [aɪˈdiːəl] 49 ideal
if [ɪf] 28 wenn, falls
important [ɪmˈpɔːtnt] 12 wichtig
in pairs [ɪn ˈpeəz] 31 paarweise
independence [ˌɪndɪˈpendəns] 30 Unabhängigkeit
independent(ly) [ˌɪndɪˈpendəntli] 43 selbstständig
information [ˌɪnfəˈmeɪʃn] 36 Angaben, Informationen
ingredient [ɪnˈɡriːdiənt] 24 Zutat
inside [ɪnˈsaɪd] 29 in, innen, darin, im Inneren; 30 hinein; 33 drinnen
instead [ɪnˈsted] 24 stattdessen
instructions *pl* [ɪnˈstrʌkʃnz] 28 Anweisungen
interested: to be interested in sth [bi ˈɪntrəstɪd ɪn] 57 an etw interessiert sein
interesting [ˈɪntrəstɪŋ] 46 interessant
intern [ˈɪntɜːn] 51 Praktikant/in
internship [ˈɪntɜːnʃɪp] 51 Praktikum
interview [ˈɪntəvjuː] 59 Vorstellungsgespräch
to introduce oneself [ˌɪntrəˈdjuːs wʌnself] 57 sich vorstellen
to invite sb [ɪnˈvaɪt] 24 jdn einladen
it [ɪt] 3 es
item [ˈaɪtəm] 25 Artikel, Gegenstand

J

jacket [ˈdʒækɪt] 33 Jacke
jam [dʒæm] 29 Marmelade, Konfitüre
January [ˈdʒænjuəri] 30 Januar
job [dʒɒb] 41 Beruf, Stelle, Job
job ad/advert [ˈdʒɒb æd/ædvɜːt] 54 Stellenanzeige
job interview [ˈdʒɒb ɪntəvjuː] 59 Vorstellungsgespräch
to join: to join sb [dʒɔɪn] 53 zu jdm kommen, bei jdm mitmachen
to join in the fun [dʒɔɪn ˌɪn ðə ˈfʌn] 32 mitmachen
juice [dʒuːs] 29 Saft
July [dʒuˈlaɪ] 30 Juli
June [dʒuːn] 30 Juni
just [dʒʌst] 25 nur
just here [ˌdʒʌst ˈhɪə] 25 genau hier

K

key [kiː] 48 Schlüssel
kind [kaɪnd] 12 freundlich, nett, lieb; 23 Art, Sorte
kindergarten [ˈkɪndəɡɑːtn] 41 Kindergarten
kindergarten teacher [ˈkɪndəɡɑːtn tiːtʃə] 41 Kindergärtner/in, Erzieher/in
kitchen [ˈkɪtʃɪn] 35 Küche
to know [nəʊ] 13 wissen
knowledge: basic knowledge [ˌbeɪsɪk ˈnɒlɪdʒ] 58 Grundkenntnisse

L

laboratory [ləˈbɒrətri] 41 Labor
laboratory assistant [ləˈbɒrətri əsɪstənt] 41 Laborant/in
lake [leɪk] 34 See
by the lake [baɪ ðə ˈleɪk] 35 am See
lakeside [ˈleɪksaɪd] 35 am See, am Seeufer

tʃ	dʒ	ʃ	ʒ	θ	ð	ŋ	s	z	v	w
chip	jet	ship	garage	thing	the	ring	ice	as	very	wet

lamb [læm] 21 Lamm
language [ˈlæŋgwɪdʒ] 58 Sprache
large [lɑːdʒ] 35 groß, geräumig
lasagna [ləˈzɑːnjə] 22 Lasagne
last [lɑːst] 32 letzte/r/s
last name [ˈlɑːst neɪm] 36 Nachname
late [leɪt] 44 spät, zu spät
later [ˈleɪtə] 15 später, nachher
to laugh [lɑːf] 12 lachen
to make sb laugh [ˌmeɪk ˈlɑːf] 12 jdn zum Lachen bringen
lazy [ˈleɪzi] 18 faul
leading [ˈliːdɪŋ] 55 führend
to leave a message [ˌliːv ə ˈmesɪdʒ] 17 eine Nachricht hinterlassen
left [left] 44 links, linke/r/s
on the left [ɒn ðə ˈleft] 44 links, auf der linken Seite
lemon [ˈlemən] 23 Zitrone
lemonade [ˌleməˈneɪd] 24 Limonade
Let's (= let us) … [lets] 4 Lass(t) uns …
letter [ˈletə] 30 Buchstabe; [ˈletə] 42 Brief
level [ˈlevl] 50 Niveau, Grad
life [laɪf] 13 Leben
light [laɪt] 33 Licht
like [laɪk] 14 wie
What's he like? [ˌwɒts hiː ˈlaɪk] 13 Wie ist er denn so?
to like: to like sb/sth [laɪk] 6 jdn/etw mögen
I would like to … [ˌaɪ wʊd ˈlaɪk tə] 16 Ich möchte …; Ich würde gern …
to listen (to sth) [ˈlɪsn tə] 3 hören, zuhören, sich etw anhören
to live [lɪv] 3 leben, wohnen
local [ˈləʊkl] 35 örtlich, lokal, einheimisch
long [lɒŋ] 45 lang
look: to have a look [həv ə ˈlʊk] 27 sich etw ansehen
to look [lʊk] 5 sehen, schauen; 23 aussehen
to look after sb/sth [ˌlʊk ˈɑːftə] 43 sich um jdn/etw kümmern, sich mit jdm/etw befassen
to look at sth [ˈlʊk ət] 31 sich etw ansehen
to look for sth [ˈlʊk fə] 51 etw suchen
to look forward to sth [ˌlʊk ˈfɔːwəd tə] 57 sich auf etw freuen
to look out of the window [lʊk ˌaʊt əv ðə ˈwɪndəʊ] 5 aus dem Fenster schauen
lorry *BE* [ˈlɒri] 41 Lastwagen, Lkw
lot: a lot [ə ˈlɒt] 4 viel
a lot of [ə ˈlɒt əv] 13 viele
lots of [ˈlɒts əv] 25 viele
loud [laʊd] 15 laut
to love [lʌv] 3 lieben, (sehr) mögen
luck [lʌk] 8 Glück
Good luck! [ˌgʊd ˈlʌk] 8 Viel Glück!
lunch [lʌntʃ] 33 Mittagessen

M

machine [məˈʃiːn] 52 Maschine
to make sth [meɪk] 10 etw machen
to make sb do sth [ˌmeɪk ˈduː] 12 jdn dazu bringen, etw zu tun
to make sb laugh [ˌmeɪk ˈlɑːf] 12 jdn zum Lachen bringen
man, men [mæn, men] 45 Mann, Männer
to manage sth [ˈmænɪdʒ] 53 etw verwalten, etw leiten
manager [ˈmænɪdʒə] 54 Leiter/in
many [ˈmeni] 11 viele
how many? [haʊ ˈmeni] 11 wie viel(e)?
maple syrup [ˌmeɪpl ˈsɪrəp] 29 Ahornsirup
March [mɑːtʃ] 30 März
to match [mætʃ] 5 zuordnen
May [meɪ] 30 Mai
maybe [ˈmeɪbi] 35 vielleicht
me [miː] 7 mich, ich
Me too. [ˌmiː ˈtuː] 7 Ich auch.
meal [miːl] 35 Mahlzeit, Essen
meat [miːt] 21 Fleisch
mechanic [mɪˈkænɪk] 41 Mechaniker/in
medical [ˈmedɪkl] 53 medizinisch
to meet [miːt] 15 sich treffen
melon [ˈmelən] 21 Melone
menu [ˈmenjuː] 29 Speisekarte
message [ˈmesɪdʒ] 17 Nachricht
to leave a message [ˌliːv ə ˈmesɪdʒ] 17 eine Nachricht hinterlassen
metal worker [ˈmetl wɜːkə] 41 Metallarbeiter/in
middle [ˈmɪdl] 48 mittlere/r/s
milk [mɪlk] 9 Milch
millionaire [ˌmɪljəˈneə] 60 Millionär/in
mind map [ˈmaɪnd mæp] 42 Mindmap
mineral water [ˈmɪnərəl wɔːtə] 26 Mineralwasser
mint [mɪnt] 23 Minze
mint tea [mɪnt ˈtiː] 23 Minztee
minute [ˈmɪnɪt] 28 Minute
for 20 minutes [fə ˌtwenti ˈmɪnɪts] 28 20 Minuten (lang)
to miss sb/sth [mɪs] 23 jdn/etw vermissen; 44 jdn/etw verpassen
missing [ˈmɪsɪŋ] 30 fehlend
mix [mɪks] 29 Zusammenstellung
to mix sth [mɪks] 28 etw mischen, etw (miteinander) vermischen
mixture [ˈmɪkstʃə] 28 Mischung
modern [ˈmɒdn] 53 modern
Monday [ˈmʌndeɪ] 16 Montag
money [ˈmʌni] 15 Geld
month [mʌnθ] 30 Monat
more [mɔː] 14 mehr
more than [ˈmɔː ðən] 15 mehr als
no … more [ˌnəʊ ˈmɔː] 9 kein/e … mehr
morning [ˈmɔːnɪŋ] 4 Morgen
the most [ðə ˈməʊst] 31 die meisten
motivated [ˈməʊtɪveɪtɪd] 53 motiviert
to move [muːv] 62 sich bewegen
to move sth [muːv] 62 etw bewegen
movie [ˈmuːvi] 14 Film, Spielfilm
much [mʌtʃ] 47 viel
too much [ˌtuː ˈmʌtʃ] 21 zu viel
museum [mjuˈziːəm] 35 Museum
music [ˈmjuːzɪk] 3 Musik
musician [mjuːˈzɪʃn] 30 Musiker/in
my [maɪ] 7 mein

N

name [neɪm] 8 Name
last name [ˈlɑːst neɪm] 36 Nachname
What's your name? [ˌwɒts jɔː ˈneɪm] 8 Wie heißen Sie / heißt du?
national park [ˌnæʃnəl ˈpɑːk] 34 Nationalpark
native language [ˌneɪtɪv ˈlæŋgwɪdʒ] 59 Muttersprache
native speaker [ˌneɪtɪv ˈspiːkə] 58 Muttersprachler/in
nature [ˈneɪtʃə] 35 Natur
near [nɪə] 35 nahe, in der Nähe von
to need sth [niːd] 25 etw brauchen, etw benötigen
needs *pl* [niːdz] 53 Bedürfnisse
nervous [ˈnɜːvəs] 45 aufgeregt, nervös
never [ˈnevə] 14 nie, niemals
new [njuː] 8 neu
New Year [njuː ˈjɪə] 31 Neujahr
New Year's Eve [ˌnjuː jɪəz ˈiːv] 31 Silvester
newspaper [ˈnjuːzpeɪpə] 57 Zeitung
next to [ˈnekst tə] 25 neben
nice [naɪs] 3 nett, schön, gut
Nice to meet you. [ˌnaɪs tə ˈmiːt ju] 3 Schön, Sie/dich kennenzulernen!
night [naɪt] 30 Abend, Nacht
no [ˈnəʊ] 3 nein; 16 kein
no … more [ˌnəʊ ˈmɔː] 9 kein/e … mehr
noise [nɔɪz] 41 Geräusch
noodles *pl* [ˈnuːdlz] 29 Nudeln
not [nɒt] 3 nicht
note [nəʊt] 26 Geldschein, Banknote
notepad [ˈnəʊtpæd] 48 Notizblock
notice board [ˈnəʊtɪsbɔːd] 57 Schwarzes Brett

iː	ɪ	e	æ	ɑː	ɒ	ɔː	ʊ	uː	ʌ	ɜː	ə	i	u
see	in	yes	apple	car	got	or	put	too	cut	girl	sister	happy	you

November [nəʊˈvembə] 30 November
now [naʊ] 3 jetzt
number [ˈnʌmbə] 8 Nummer; 25 Zahl; 36 Anzahl

O

October [ɒkˈtəʊbə] 30 Oktober
of [əv] 11 von
of course [əf ˈkɔːs] 12 natürlich, selbstverständlich
off: 25% off [ɒf] 26 25% weniger, um 25% reduziert
to offer sb sth [ˈɒfə] 46 jdm etw anbieten
office [ˈɒfɪs] 8 Büro
office assistant [ˈɒfɪs əsɪstənt] 58 Büroassistent/in, Sekretär/in
office suppliers *pl* [ˈɒfɪs səplaɪəz] 54 Fachhandel für Bürobedarf
office worker [ˈɒfɪs wɜːkə] 41 Büroangestellte/r
often [ˈɒfn] 21 oft, häufig
oil [ɔɪl] 21 Öl
old [əʊld] 18 alt
olive [ˈɒlɪv] 24 Olive
on [ɒn] 11 an, auf
on the left/right [ɒn ðə ˈleft/raɪt] 44 links/rechts, auf der linken/rechten Seite
on Fridays [ɒn ˈfraɪdeɪz] 37 freitags
on holiday [ɒn ˈhɒlədeɪ] 35 im Urlaub
on-the-job training [ɒn ðə ˌdʒɒb ˈtreɪnɪŋ] 53 Ausbildung am Arbeitsplatz
one [wʌn] 11 ein/e, eins
onion [ˈʌnjən] 23 Zwiebel
online [ˈɒnlaɪn] 16 online
only [ˈəʊnli] 35 nur
the only [ði ˈəʊnli] 31 der/die/das einzige
open [ˈəʊpən] 12 offen
opportunity [ˌɒpəˈtjuːnəti] 53 Gelegenheit, Möglichkeit
or [ɔː] 6 oder
orange [ˈɒrɪndʒ] 23 Apfelsine, Orange
to order [ˈɔːdə] 29 bestellen
order [ˈɔːdə] 17 Reihenfolge
to put sth in the right order [ˌpʊt ɪn ðə ˌraɪt ˈɔːdə] 17 etw in die richtige Reihenfolge bringen
to organize sth [ˈɔːgənaɪz] 43 etw organisieren
original [əˈrɪdʒənl] 38 echt, original
other [ˈʌðə] 12 andere/r/s
our [ˈaʊə] 17 unser/e
out (of) [ˈaʊt əv] 5 aus (heraus)
outside [ˌaʊtˈsaɪd] 43 draußen; 55 außerhalb von
over there [ˌəʊvə ˈðeə] 25 da drüben
own [əʊn] 29 eigene/r/s

P

p.m. [ˌpiː ˈem] 16 *(Uhrzeit:)* nachmittags, abends
packet [ˈpækɪt] 25 Packung
to paint [peɪnt] 41 malen
painter [ˈpeɪntə] 41 Maler/in, Dekorateur/in
pair [peə] 31 Paar
in pairs [ɪn ˈpeəz] 31 paarweise
palace [ˈpæləs] 38 Palast, Schloss
pancake [ˈpænkeɪk] 28 Pfannkuchen
paper [ˈpeɪpə] 33 Papier
piece of paper [piːs əf ˈpeɪpə] 33 Blatt Papier, Zettel
parade [pəˈreɪd] 30 Umzug, Parade
parents *pl* [ˈpeərənts] 59 Eltern
park [pɑːk] 7 Park
parking [ˈpɑːkɪŋ] 34 Parkplatz
part [pɑːt] 33 Teil
part-time [ˌpɑːtˈtaɪm] 44 Teilzeit-
partner [ˈpɑːtnə] 4 Partner/in
party [ˈpɑːti] 4 Feier, Party
to pass sb sth [pɑːs] 29 jdm etw reichen, jdm etw geben
patient [ˈpeɪʃnt] 52 Patient/in; 56 geduldig
payment [ˈpeɪmənt] 42 Zahlung
pea [piː] 28 Erbse
pen [pen] 47 Stift
pencil [ˈpensl] 48 Bleistift
pencil case [ˈpensl keɪs] 48 Federmäppchen, Stiftetui
penny, pence [ˈpeni, pens] 26 Penny, Pence
people [ˈpiːpl] 4 (die) Leute, man; 17 Personen
pepper [ˈpepə] 21 Paprika
per [pə] 35 pro
perfect [ˈpɜːfɪkt] 11 perfekt
person [ˈpɜːsn] 12 Mensch, Person
per person [ˌpɜː ˈpɜːsn] 35 pro Person
personal [ˈpɜːsənl] 56 persönlich
pet [pet] 15 Haustier
phone [fəʊn] 15 Telefon;
to talk on the phone [ˌtɔːk ɒn ðə ˈfəʊn] 15 telefonieren
phone number [ˈfəʊn nʌmbə] 17 Telefonnummer
to phone sb [fəʊn] 17 jdn anrufen
photo [ˈfəʊtəʊ] 18 Foto, Bild
to take a photo [ˌteɪk ə ˈfəʊtəʊ] 38 ein Foto/Bild machen
photocopier [ˈfəʊtəʊkɒpiə] 47 Fotokopierer
physical(ly) [ˈfɪzɪkl] 56 körperlich
picnic [ˈpɪknɪk] 14 Picknick
picture [ˈpɪktʃə] 6 Bild
place [pleɪs] 34 Ort
place to stay [ˌpleɪs tə ˈsteɪ] 34 Unterkunft, Übernachtungsmöglichkeit
plan [plæn] 47 Plan
to plan sth [plæn] 25 etw planen
plane [pleɪn] 36 Flugzeug
plant [plɑːnt] 48 Pflanze
platform [ˈplætfɔːm] 36 Bahnsteig
to play [pleɪ] 7 spielen
please [pliːz] 8 bitte
point [pɔɪnt] 11 Punkt
police officer [pəˈliːs ɒfɪsə] 41 Polizeibeamter/-beamtin
polite [pəˈlaɪt] 56 höflich
politics [ˈpɒlətɪks] 4 Politik
popular [ˈpɒpjələ] 23 beliebt, populär
pork [pɔːk] 21 Schweinefleisch
position [pəˈzɪʃn] 52 Stelle
positive [ˈpɒzətɪv] 13 positiv
possible [ˈpɒsəbl] 55 möglich
postal worker [ˌpəʊstl ˈwɜːkə] 41 Postangestellte/r, Zustelle/r
postcode [ˈpəʊstkəʊd] 8 Postleitzahl
poster [ˈpəʊstə] 10 Plakat
potato [pəˈteɪtəʊ] 21 Kartoffel
pound [paʊnd] 9 Pfund
powder [ˈpaʊdə] 28 Pulver
practical [ˈpræktɪkl] 43 praktisch
prediction [prɪˈdɪkʃn] 60 Voraussage
to prepare sth [prɪˈpeə] 53 etw vorbereiten
present [ˈpreznt] 30 Geschenk
to present sb/sth to sb [prɪˈzent tə] 18 jdn/etw jdm vorstellen
pressure [ˈpreʃə] 55 Druck
price [praɪs] 26 Preis
private [ˈpraɪvət] 34 privat
probably [ˈprɒbəbli] 29 wahrscheinlich
problem [ˈprɒbləm] 12 Problem
No problem! [nəʊ ˈprɒbləm] 16 Kein Problem!
product [ˈprɒdʌkt] 25 Produkt
pub [pʌb] 33 Kneipe, Pub
pumpkin [ˈpʌmpkɪn] 30 Kürbis
punch: hole punch [ˈhəʊl pʌntʃ] 48 Locher
punctual [ˈpʌŋktʃuəl] 56 pünktlich
to put [pʊt] 17 setzen, stellen, legen
to put sth in/on sth [ˈpʊt ɪn/ɒn] 29 etw in/auf etw tun
to put sth into sth [ˈpʊt ɪntə] 28 etw in etw (hinein)tun
to put sth in the right order [ˌpʊt ɪn ðə ˌraɪt ˈɔːdə] 17 etw in die richtige Reihenfolge bringen

Q

quality [ˈkwɒləti] 56 Eigenschaft
question [ˈkwestʃən] 13 Frage
quick(ly) [ˈkwɪkli] 55 schnell

tʃ	dʒ	ʃ	ʒ	θ	ð	ŋ	s	z	v	w
chip	jet	ship	garage	thing	the	ring	ice	as	very	wet

R

rainy ['reɪni] 5 regnerisch
raisin ['reɪzn] 29 Rosine
to read [ri:d] 3 lesen
to read sth out [ˌri:d 'aʊt] 12 etw vorlesen
really ['ri:əli] 4 wirklich, tatsächlich
reception [rɪ'sepʃn] 46 Empfang, Rezeption
reception desk [rɪ'sepʃn desk] 55 Empfangsschalter
recipe ['resəpi] 28 (Koch-)Rezept
red [red] 21 rot
registration [ˌredʒɪ'streɪʃn] 8 Anmeldung
to relax [rɪ'læks] 9 sich ausruhen, sich entspannen, sich erholen
relevant ['reləvənt] 57 entsprechend, relevant
reliable [rɪ'laɪəbl] 58 zuverlässig
religion [rɪ'lɪdʒən] 4 Religion
to repair sth [rɪ'peə] 41 etw reparieren
to repeat sth [rɪ'pi:t] 26 etw wiederholen
research [rɪ'sɜ:tʃ] 53 Forschung(en)
rest [rest] 48 Rest
restaurant ['restrɒnt] 7 Restaurant
résumé *AE* [rɪ'zju:m] 54 Lebenslauf
rice [raɪs] 21 Reis
right [raɪt] 13 richtig; 46 rechts, rechte/r/s
That's right. [ˌðæts 'raɪt] 26 Das stimmt.
on the right [ɒn ðə 'raɪt] 46 rechts, auf der rechten Seite
right? [raɪt] 21 nicht wahr?, oder?
to be right [bi 'raɪt] 15 recht haben
road [rəʊd] 8 Straße
role-play ['rəʊlpleɪ] 9 Rollenspiel
roll [rəʊl] 27 Brötchen
room [ru:m] 34 Zimmer
to run [rʌn] 45 laufen

S

safe(ly) ['seɪfli] 56 sicher
salad ['sæləd] 21 Salat
sales assistant ['seɪlz əsɪstənt] 41 Verkäufer/in
salt [sɔ:lt] 28 Salz
salty ['sɔ:lti] 22 salzig
same: exactly the same [ɪgˌzæktli ðə 'seɪm] 23 genauso, genau gleich
Saturday ['sætədeɪ] 16 Samstag, Sonnabend
sauce [sɔ:s] 22 Soße
sausage ['sɒsɪdʒ] 23 Wurst, Bratwurst
to save sth [seɪv] 26 etw sparen
savoury ['seɪvəri] 29 salzig, pikant
to say [seɪ] 12 sagen
to say hello to sb [ˌseɪ hə'ləʊ tə] 38 jdn begrüßen, jdm guten Tag sagen
to say sorry [seɪ 'sɒri] 46 sich entschuldigen
scary ['skeəri] 30 gruselig, furchteinflößend
school [sku:l] 8 Schule
to finish school [ˌfɪnɪʃ 'sku:l] 51 die Schule beenden, den Schulabschluss machen
to leave school [li:v 'sku:l] 59 von der Schule abgehen, den Schulabschluss machen
scissors *pl* ['sɪzəz] 48 Schere
secretary ['sekrətri] 8 Sekretär/in
secretary's office [ˌsekrətriz 'ɒfɪs] 8 Sekretariat
to see [si:] 16 sehen
See you later. [ˌsi: ju 'leɪtə] 24 Bis später! Bis nachher!
See you on ... ! ['si: ju: ɒn] 16 Bis ... !
See you soon! [ˌsi: ju 'su:n] 27 Bis bald!
See you then! [ˌsi: ju: 'ðen] 16 Bis dann!
to sell [sel] 41 verkaufen
to send sth [send] 24 etw schicken
sentence ['sentəns] 7 Satz
September [sep'tembə] 30 September
to serve sb [sɜ:v] 42 jdn bedienen
to serve sth [sɜ:v] 42 etw servieren
serviette *BE* [ˌsɜ:vi'et] 46 Serviette
shall [ʃəl] 24 sollen
shared [ʃeəd] 34 gemeinsam genutzt, Gemeinschafts-
she [ʃi:] 12 sie
shelf [ʃelf] 48 Regal
shisha [ˌʃi:ʃə] 15 Wasserpfeife
shop [ʃɒp] 27 Laden, Geschäft
shop assistant ['ʃɒp əsɪstənt] 27 Verkäufer/in
shopping ['ʃɒpɪŋ] 3 Einkaufen
to go shopping [gəʊ 'ʃɒpɪŋ] 27 einkaufen gehen
shopping list ['ʃɒpɪŋ lɪst] 24 Einkaufsliste
short [ʃɔ:t] 52 kurz
to show sb sth [ʃəʊ] 29 jdm etw zeigen
shower ['ʃaʊə] 15 Dusche
sick [sɪk] 4 krank
to sing [sɪŋ] 14 singen
singer ['sɪŋə] 20 Sänger/in
single room [ˌsɪŋgl 'ru:m] 34 Einzelzimmer
sister ['sɪstə] 18 Schwester
to sit down [ˌsɪt 'daʊn] 8 Platz nehmen, sich setzen
skill [skɪl] 50 Fähigkeit, Fertigkeit
sky [skaɪ] 38 Himmel
to sleep [sli:p] 3 schlafen
sleep [sli:p] 15 Schlaf
small [smɔ:l] 33 klein
small talk ['smɔ:l tɔ:k] 4 höfliche Konversation, Smalltalk
to smile [smaɪl] 12 lächeln
to smoke [sməʊk] 15 rauschen
snake [sneɪk] 42 Schlange
snowy: It is snowy. [ˌɪt ɪz 'snəʊi] 5 Es schneit.
so [səʊ] 4 so
social ['səʊʃl] 53 sozial
some [sʌm] 14 einige, ein paar, etwas
something ['sʌmθɪŋ] 25 etwas
sometimes ['sʌmtaɪmz] 14 manchmal
son [sʌn] 18 Sohn
song [sɒŋ] 7 Lied
Sorry. ['sɒri] 11 Tut mir leid! Entschuldigung!
to say sorry [seɪ 'sɒri] 46 sich entschuldigen
to sound [saʊnd] 12 klingen, sich anhören
sour ['saʊə] 22 sauer
sour cream [ˌsaʊə 'kri:m] 29 saure Sahne
south [saʊθ] 29 Süden, Süd-
to speak (to sb) [spi:k] 14 (mit jdm) sprechen
special ['speʃl] 31 besondere/r/s, speziell
special offer [ˌspeʃl 'ɒfə] 26 Sonderangebot
speech bubble ['spi:tʃ bʌbl] 12 Sprechblase
to spell [spel] 8 buchstabieren
to spend money on sth [ˌspend 'mʌni ɒn] 15 Geld für etw ausgeben
spicy ['spaɪsi] 15 würzig, scharf, pikant
to spill sth [spɪl] 44 etw verschütten
spinach ['spɪnɪtʃ] 29 Spinat
sport: to do sport [du 'spɔ:t] 11 Sport treiben
spring [sprɪŋ] 30 Frühling
stadium ['steɪdiəm] 14 Stadion
to stand [stænd] 31 stehen, sich stellen
standard ['stændəd] 53 Norm, Vorschrift
stapler ['steɪplə] 48 Hefter
to start [stɑ:t] 35 beginnen, starten
station ['steɪʃn] 37 Bahnhof
stationery ['steɪʃənri] 47 Schreibwaren, Bürpbedarf
to stay [steɪ] 13 bleiben; 34 übernachten
stew [stju:] 33 Eintopf, Schmorgericht
sticky note ['stɪki nəʊt] 48 Haftnotiz
store [stɔ:] 53 Laden, Geschäft

i:	ɪ	e	æ	ɑ:	ɒ	ɔ:	ʊ	u:	ʌ	ɜ:	ə	i	u
see	in	yes	apple	car	got	or	put	too	cut	girl	sister	happy	you

story [ˈstɔ:ri] 43 Geschichte
straight on [ˌstreɪt ˈɒn] 46 geradeaus
strawberry [ˈstrɔ:bəri] 21 Erdbeere
street [stri:t] 30 Straße
strength [streŋθ] 56 Stärke
stressed [strest] 45 gestresst
strong [strɒŋ] 56 stark, kräftig
student [ˈstju:dnt] 8 Schüler/in
student [ˈstju:dnt] 37 Student/in, Schüler/in
style [staɪl] 56 Stil
subject [ˈsʌbdʒɪkt] 57 Thema, *(Brief:)* Betreff
sugar [ˈʃʊgə] 21 Zucker
summer [ˈsʌmə] 10 Sommer
Sunday [ˈsʌndeɪ] 16 Sonntag
sunflower [ˈsʌnflaʊə] 28 Sonnenblume
sunflower oil [ˈsʌnflaʊər ɔɪl] 28 Sonnenblumenöl
sunny [ˈsʌni] 5 sonnig
supermarket [ˈsu:pəmɑ:kɪt] 14 Supermarkt
to supply sb with sth [səˈplaɪ wɪð] 55 jdn mit etw beliefern
sure [ʃʊə] 17 sicher
Sure! [ʃʊə] 17 Na klar!
to swap [swɒp] 3 tauschen
sweet [swi:t] 22 süß
sweets *pl* [swi:ts] 25 Süßigkeiten
to swim [swɪm] 14 schwimmen
swimming, to go swimming [gəʊ ˈswɪmɪŋ] 14 schwimmen gehen
swimming pool [ˈswɪmɪŋ pu:l] 14 Schwimmbad

T

table [ˈteɪbl] 16 Tisch
tailor [ˈteɪlə] 41 Schneider/in
to take sth [teɪk] 33 etw nehmen
to take an order [ˌteɪk ən ˈɔ:də] 58 eine Bestellung aufnehmen
takeaway [ˈteɪkəweɪ] 38 Essen zum Mitnehmen
to talk (to sb) [tɔ:k] 3 (mit jdm) sprechen, (mit jdm) reden
task [tɑ:sk] 53 Aufgabe
to do a task [ˌdu: ə ˈtɑ:sk] 53 eine Aufgabe erledigen
to taste [teɪst] 22 schmecken
tasty [ˈteɪsti] 22 lecker
taxi driver [ˈtæksi draɪvə] 41 Taxifahrer/in
tea [ti:] 9 Tee
cup of tea [kʌp əf ˈti:] 11 Tasse Tee;
mint tea [mɪnt ˈti:] 23 Minztee
to teach sb sth [ti:tʃ] 14 jdm etw beibringen
teacher [ˈti:tʃə] 20 Lehrer/in
team [ti:m] 53 Mannschaft, Team
technical [ˈteknɪkl] 53 technisch
telephone [ˈtelɪfəʊn] 8 Telefon
to tell [tel] 12 erzählen, berichten
tent [tent] 35 Zelt
to test sth [test] 41 etw prüfen
than [ðən] 15 als
more than [ˈmɔ: ðən] 15 mehr als
to thank sb [θæŋk] 8 jdm danken
Thank you. [ˈθæŋk ju:] 8 Vielen Dank!
Thank you very much. [ˌθæŋk ju ˌveri ˈmʌtʃ] 17 Vielen Dank!
thanks [θæŋks] 4 danke
that [ðæt] 8 das
That's … [ðæts] 9 Das kostet … ; Das macht …
That's right. [ˌðæts ˈraɪt] 26 Das stimmt.
that's why [ˈðæts waɪ] 32 deshalb, daher
the [ðə, ði] 3 der/die/das
then [ðen] 8 dann, anschließend
there [ðeə] 14 dort
there is/are … [ðeər ˈɪz/ˈɑ:] 12 es gibt …
they [ðeɪ] 13 sie
thing [θɪŋ] 12 Sache, Ding
to think [θɪŋk] 11 glauben, denken
thirsty [ˈθɜ:sti] 22 durstig
to be thirsty [bi ˈθɜ:sti] 22 Durst haben
this [ðɪs] 7 dies, diese/r/s
this time [ðɪs ˈtaɪm] 50 diesmal, dieses Mal
those [ðəʊz] 29 diese
though [ðəʊ] 25 aber, allerdings
to throw [θrəʊ] 28 werfen
Thursday [ˈθɜ:zdeɪ] 16 Donnerstag
to tick sth [tɪk] 10 etw abhaken, etw mit einem Häkchen versehen
ticket [ˈtɪkɪt] 20 (Eintritts-, Fahr-) Karte
tiger [ˈtaɪgə] 18 Tiger
time [taɪm] 6 Zeit
tinned food [ˌtɪnd ˈfu:d] 25 Lebensmittelkonserven
tinned tomatoes *pl* [ˌtɪnd təˈmɑ:təʊz] 25 Tomatenkonserven
tired [ˈtaɪəd] 33 müde, erschöpft
to [tə, tʊ, tu:] 3 zu
today [təˈdeɪ] 4 heute
tomato [təˈmɑ:təʊ] 22 Tomate
tomorrow [təˈmɒrəʊ] 16 morgen
tonight [təˈnaɪt] 25 heute Abend
too [tu:] 4 auch, ebenso
Me too. [ˌmi: ˈtu:] 7 Ich auch.
You too. [ˌju: ˈtu:] 4 Ebenso! *(als Antwort)*
too much [ˌtu: ˈmʌtʃ] 21 zu viel
tool [tu:l] 41 Werkzeug
top [tɒp] 48 oberste/r/s
from the top [frəm ðə ˈtɒp] 38 von oben
topic [ˈtɒpɪk] 4 Thema
tour [tʊə] 26 Rundfahrt
town [taʊn] 35 Stadt
old town [ˈəʊld taʊn] 35 Altstadt
trade [treɪd] 53 Handwerk
tradesperson [ˈtreɪdzpɜ:sn] 41 Handwerker/in
traditional [trəˈdɪʃənl] 30 traditionell
train [treɪn] 36 Zug
train system [ˈtreɪn sɪstəm] 38 Bahnnetz
train time [ˈtreɪn taɪm] 36 Abfahrtszeit *(eines Zuges)*
transport [ˈtrænspɔ:t] 55 Beförderung
to travel [ˈtrævl] 37 reisen, fahren
traveller [ˈtrævələ] 35 Reisende/r
tree [tri:] 30 Baum
truck *AE* [trʌk] 41 Lastwagen, Lkw
true [tru:] 15 wahr, richtig, zutreffend
to try sth [traɪ] 29 etw versuchen, etw probieren
the Tube [ðə tju:b] 38 *Londoner U-Bahn*
Tuesday [ˈtju:zdeɪ] 16 Dienstag
to turn to page 52 [ˈtɜ:n tə peɪdʒ] 4 Seite 52 aufschlagen
to type [taɪp] 42 tippen
typical [ˈtɪpɪkl] 29 typisch

U

uncle [ˈʌŋkl] 13 Onkel
under [ˈʌndə] 30 unter
underground [ˈʌndəgraʊnd] 38 unterirdisch, U-Bahn
to understand [ˌʌndəˈstænd] 46 verstehen
uniform [ˈju:nɪfɔ:m] 59 Dienstkleidung
until [ənˈtɪl] 37 bis
us [ʌs] 4 uns
usually [ˈju:ʒuəli] 51 üblicherweise, normalerweise

V

van [væn] 41 Lieferwagen
vegan [ˈvi:gən] 21 Veganer/in, vegan
vegetable [ˈvedʒtəbl] 21 Gemüse
vegetarian [ˌvedʒəˈteəriən] 21 Vegetarier/in, vegetarisch
very [ˈveri] 12 sehr
to visit sb [ˈvɪzɪt] 32 jdn besuchen
vocational college [vəʊˌkeɪʃənl ˈkɒlɪdʒ] 51 Berufsschule, Berufsfachschule
vocational school [vəʊˌkeɪʃənl ˈsku:l] 8 Berufsschule

tʃ	dʒ	ʃ	ʒ	θ	ð	ŋ	s	z	v	w
chip	jet	ship	garage	thing	the	ring	ice	as	very	wet

W

waiter [ˈweɪtə] 41 Kellner
waitress [ˈweɪtrɪs] 41 Kellnerin
to wake up [ˌweɪk ˈʌp] 35 aufwachen
to walk [wɔːk] 33 laufen, gehen, spazieren gehen
walk [wɔːk] 35 Fußweg, Spaziergang
walking distance [ˈwɔːkɪŋ dɪstəns] 38 (in) Gehweite
to want [wɒnt] 7 wollen
wanted [ˈwɒntɪd] 53 gesucht
to warm up [ˌwɔːm ˈʌp] 3 sich aufwärmen, sich warm machen
to warm sth up [ˌwɔːm ˈʌp] 28 etw warm machen, etw heiß werden lassen
to wash [wɒʃ] 42 waschen
to watch sth [wɒtʃ] 14 (sich) etw ansehen
to watch TV [wɒtʃ ˌtiːˈviː] 3 fernsehen
water [ˈwɔːtə] 24 Wasser
watermelon [ˈwɔːtəmelən] 25 Wassermelone
way [weɪ] 53 Art (und Weise)
to wear sth [weə] 30 etw *(Kleidung usw.)* tragen
weather [ˈweðə] 4 Wetter
Wednesday [ˈwenzdeɪ] 16 Mittwoch
week [wiːk] 26 Woche
weekend [ˌwiːkˈend] 16 Wochenende
welcome (to sth) [ˈwelkəm tə] 3 willkommen (bei/in/auf/zu etw)
well, … [wel] 12 nun, …
what [wɒt] 5 was; 17 welche/r/s
What about … ? [ˈwɒt əbaʊt] 16 Wie wäre es mit … ?
What's the time? [wɒts ðə ˈtaɪm] 44 Wie viel Uhr ist es? Wie spät ist es?
What's your name? [ˌwɒts jɔː ˈneɪm] 8 Wie heißen Sie / heißt du?
What's that song? [ˌwɒts θæt ˈsɒŋ] 7 Welches Lied ist das?
What would you like? [ˌwɒt wʊd juː ˈlaɪk] 9 Was hätten Sie / hättest Du denn gern?
where [weə] 13 wo
where … from [ˌweə ˈfrɒm] 13 woher
which [wɪtʃ] 17 welche/r/s
white [waɪt] 30 weiß
who [huː] 3 wer
why [waɪ] 6 warum
that's why [ˈðæts waɪ] 32 deshalb, daher
willing [ˈwɪlɪŋ] 58 bereit, willig
to win [wɪn] 14 gewinnen
window [ˈwɪndəʊ] 5 Fenster
windy [ˈwɪndi] 5 windig
winner [ˈwɪnə] 11 Sieger/in, Gewinner/in
winter [ˈwɪntə] 10 Winter
with [wɪð, wɪθ] 9 mit
with sb [wɪð, wɪθ] 53 bei jdm
word [wɜːd] 6 Wort
to work [wɜːk] 11 arbeiten
work experience [ˈwɜːk ɪkspɪəriəns] 46 Praktikum
to do work experience [ˌduː ˈwɜːk ɪkspɪəriəns] 46 ein Praktikum machen
to work out [ˌwɜːk ˈaʊt] 14 trainieren
worker [ˈwɜːkə] 41 Arbeiter/in
working life [ˌwɜːkɪŋ ˈlaɪf] 41 Arbeitsleben
workshop [ˈwɜːkʃɒp] 53 Werkstatt
world [wɜːld] 26 Welt
around the world [əˌraʊnd ðə ˈwɜːld] 26 weltweit, auf der ganzen Welt
to worry [ˈwʌri] 52 sich Sorgen machen
would [wʊd] 9 würde/n
I would like to … [ˌaɪ wʊd ˈlaɪk tə] 16 Ich möchte …; Ich würde gern …
to write [raɪt] 3 schreiben
wrong [rɒŋ] 13 falsch
to be wrong [bi ˈrɒŋ] 15 unrecht haben, sich irren

Y

Yay! [jeɪ] 5 Juhu!
year [jɪə] 18 Jahr;
all year round [ˌɔːl jɪə ˈraʊnd] 30 das ganze Jahr (über)
yellow [ˈjeləʊ] 21 gelb
yes [jes] 3 ja
yesterday [ˈjestədeɪ] 32 gestern
yoghurt [ˈjɒgət] 21 Joghurt
you [juː] 3 du, Sie, ihr
You too. [ˌjuː ˈtuː] 4 Ebenso! *(als Antwort)*
young [jʌŋ] 43 jung
You're welcome. [jɔː ˈwelkəm] 25 Bitte! Bitte sehr! *(Erwiderung auf Dank)*
your [jɔː] 5 dein
Your turn! [ˈjɔː tɜːn] 10 Sie sind an der Reihe! Du bist dran!
Yours sincerely [ˌjɔːz sɪnˈsɪəli] 58 Mit freundlichen Grüßen
yum [jʌm] 7 lecker

Z

zero [ˈzɪərəʊ] 11 null

iː	ɪ	e	æ	ɑː	ɒ	ɔː	ʊ	uː	ʌ	ɜː	ə	i	u
see	in	yes	apple	car	got	or	put	too	cut	girl	sister	happy	you

COUNTRY NAMES

Afghanistan	[æf'gænɪstæn]	Afghanistan
Afghan	['æfgæn]	afghanisch
Albania	[æl'beɪniə]	Albanien
Albanian	[æl'beɪniən]	albanisch
Australia	[ɒ'streɪliə]	Australien
Australian	[ɒ'streɪliən]	australisch
Austria	['ɒstriə]	Österreich
Austrian	['ɒstriən]	österreichisch
Brazil	[brə'zɪl]	Brasilien
Brazilian	[brə'zɪliən]	brasilianisch
Britain	['brɪtn]	Großbritannien
British	['brɪtɪʃ]	britisch
Canada	['kænədə]	Kanada
Canadian	[kə'neɪdiən]	Kanada
Caribbean	[ˌkærə'bi:ən]	karibisch
China	[tʃaɪ'nə]	China
Chinese	[tʃaɪ'ni:z]	chinesisch
Colombia	[kə'lɒmbiə]	Kolumbien
Colombian	[kə'lɒmbiən]	kolumbianisch
Croatia	[krəʊ'eɪʃə]	Kroatien
Croatian	[krəʊ'eɪʃən]	kroatisch
Ethiopia	[ˌi:θi'əʊpiə]	Äthiopien
Ethiopian	[ˌi:θi'əʊpiən]	äthiopisch
France	[frɑ:ns]	Frankreich
French	[frentʃ]	französisch
German	['dʒɜ:mən]	deutsch
Germany	['dʒɜ:məni]	Deutschland
India	['ɪndiə]	Indien
Indian	['ɪndiən]	indisch
Iraq	[ɪ'rɑ:k]	Irak
Ireland	['aɪələnd]	Irland
Irish	['aɪrɪʃ]	irisch
Italy	['ɪtəli]	Italien
Italian	[ɪ'tæljən]	italienisch
Japan	[dʒə'pæn]	Japan
Japanese	[ˌdʒæpə'ni:z]	Japan
Mexico	['meksɪkəʊ]	Mexiko
Mexican	['meksɪkən]	mexikanisch
Nigeria	[naɪ'dʒɪəriə]	Nigeria
Nigerian	[naɪ'dʒɪəriən]	nigerianisch
Pakistan	[ˌpɑ:kɪ'stɑ:n]	Pakistan
Pakistani	[ˌpɑ:kɪ'stɑ:ni]	pakistanisch
Poland	['pəʊlənd]	Polen
Polish	['pəʊlɪʃ]	polnisch
Romania	[ru:'meɪniə]	Rumänien
Romanian	[ru:'meɪniən]	rumänisch
Russia	['rʌʃə]	Russland
Russian	['rʌʃn]	russisch
Scotland	['skɒtlənd]	Schottland
Scottish	['skɒtɪʃ]	schottisch
South Africa	[ˌsaʊθ 'æfrɪkə]	Südafrika
South African	[ˌsaʊθ 'æfrɪkən]	südafrikanisch
Spain	[speɪn]	Spanien
Spanish	['spænɪʃ]	spanisch
Sweden	['swi:dn]	Schweden
Swedish	['swi:dɪʃ]	schwedisch
Syria	['sɪriə]	Syrien
Syrian	['sɪriən]	syrisch
Thai	[taɪ]	thailändisch
Turkey	['tɜ:ki]	Türkei
Turkish	['tɜ:kɪʃ]	türkisch
UK (United Kingdom)	[ˌju: 'keɪ, juˌnaɪtɪd 'kɪŋdəm]	Vereinigtes Königreich, Großbritannien
Ukraine	[ju:'kreɪn]	Ukraine
Ukrainian	[ju:'kreɪnɪən]	ukrainisch

NUMBERS

0	**oh, zero, nil** [əʊ, ˈzɪərəʊ, nɪl]		
1	**one** [wʌn]	1st	**first** [fɜːst]
2	**two** [tuː]	2nd	**second** [ˈsekənd]
3	**three** [θriː]	3rd	**third** [θɜːd]
4	**four** [fɔː]	4th	**fourth** [fɔːθ]
5	**five** [faɪv]	5th	**fifth** [fɪfθ]
6	**six** [sɪks]	6th	**sixth** [sɪksθ]
7	**seven** [ˈsevn]	7th	**seventh** [ˈsevnθ]
8	**eight** [eɪt]	8th	**eighth** [eɪtθ]
9	**nine** [naɪn]	9th	**ninth** [naɪnθ]
10	**ten** [ten]	10th	**tenth** [tenθ]
11	**eleven** [ɪˈlevn]	11th	**eleventh** [ɪˈlevnθ]
12	**twelve** [twelv]	12th	**twelfth** [twelfθ]
13	**thirteen** [θɜːˈtiːn]	13th	**thirteenth** [θɜːˈtiːnθ]
14	**fourteen** [fɔːˈtiːn]	14th	**fourteenth** [fɔːˈtiːnθ]
15	**fifteen** [fɪfˈtiːn]	15th	**fifteenth** [fɪfˈtiːnθ]
16	**sixteen** [sɪksˈtiːn]	16th	**sixteenth** [sɪksˈtiːnθ]
17	**seventeen** [sevnˈtiːn]	17th	**seventeenth** [sevnˈtiːnθ]
18	**eighteen** [eɪˈtiːn]	18th	**eighteenth** [eɪˈtiːnθ]
19	**nineteen** [naɪnˈtiːn]	19th	**nineteenth** [naɪnˈtiːnθ]
20	**twenty** [ˈtwenti]	20th	**twentieth** [ˈtwentiəθ]
21	**twenty-one** [twentiˈwʌn]	21st	**twenty-first** [twentiˈfɜːst]
22	**twenty-two** [twentiˈtuː]	22nd	**twenty-second** [twentiˈsekənd]
23	**twenty-three** [twentiˈθriː]	23rd	**twenty-third** [twentiˈθɜːd]
	...		...
30	**thirty** [ˈθɜːti]	30th	**thirtieth** [ˈθɜːtiəθ]
40	**forty** [ˈfɔːti]	40th	**fortieth** [ˈfɔːtiəθ]
50	**fifty** [ˈfɪfti]	50th	**fiftieth** [ˈfɪftiəθ]
60	**sixty** [ˈsɪksti]	60th	**sixtieth** [ˈsɪkstiəθ]
70	**seventy** [ˈsevnti]	70th	**seventieth** [ˈsevntiəθ]
80	**eighty** [ˈeɪti]	80th	**eightieth** [ˈeɪtiəθ]
90	**ninety** [ˈnaɪnti]	90th	**ninetieth** [ˈnaɪntiəθ]
100	**a/one hundred** [ə/wʌn ˈhʌndrəd]	100th	**hundredth** [ˈhʌndrədθ]
101	**one hundred and one**	101st	**hundred and first**
102	**one hundred and two**	102nd	**hundred and second**

Irregular verbs

Grundform	Vergangenheit	Bedeutung
be (am, are, is)	**was/were**	*sein*
bring	**brought**	*bringen*
buy	**bought**	*kaufen*
catch	**caught**	*(auf)fangen*
choose	**chose**	*(aus)wählen*
come	**came**	*kommen*
cost	**cost**	*kosten*
cut	**cut**	*schneiden*
do	**did**	*tun, machen*
draw	**drew**	*zeichnen*
drink	**drank**	*trinken*
drive	**drove**	*fahren*
eat	**ate**	*essen*
feel	**felt**	*(sich) fühlen, empfinden*
find	**found**	*finden*
forget	**forgot**	*vergessen*
get	**got**	*bekommen*
give	**gave**	*geben*
go	**went**	*gehen, fahren*
hang	**hung**	*hängen*
have (have, has)	**had**	*haben*
hear	**heard**	*hören*
know	**knew**	*kennen, wissen*
leave	**left**	*abfahren, verlassen, weggehen*
let	**let**	*lassen*
make	**made**	*machen*
meet	**met**	*treffen*
pay	**paid**	*bezahlen*
put	**put**	*setzen, stellen, legen*
read	**read**	*lesen*
run	**ran**	*laufen, rennen*
say	**said**	*sagen*
see	**saw**	*sehen*
sell	**sold**	*verkaufen*
send	**sent**	*senden, schicken*
sit	**sat**	*sitzen*
sleep	**slept**	*schlafen*
speak	**spoke**	*sprechen*
spell	**spelt/spelled**	*buchstabieren*
spend	**spent**	*ausgeben, verbringen*
sing	**sang**	*singen*
stand	**stood**	*stehen*
swim	**swam**	*schwimmen*
take	**took**	*nehmen*
teach	**taught**	*unterrichten, beibringen*
tell	**told**	*sagen, erzählen*
think	**thought**	*denken*
throw	**threw**	*werfen*
understand	**understood**	*verstehen*
wake up	**woke up**	*aufwachen*
wear	**wore**	*tragen*
win	**won**	*gewinnen*
write	**wrote**	*schreiben*

S. 3/listening Shutterstock.com/Prostock-studio; **S. 3/reading** Shutterstock.com/AlenD; **S. 3/watching TV** Shutterstock.com/Monkey Business Images; **S. 3/cooking** Shutterstock.com/Rido; **S. 3/ob. li.** Shutterstock.com/Samot; **S. 3/football** Shutterstock.com/sirtravelalot; **S. 3/dancing** Shutterstock.com/Syda Productions; **S. 3/ob. mi.** Shutterstock.com/StockImageFactory.com; **S. 3/shopping** Shutterstock.com/Octa corp; **S. 3/sleeping** Shutterstock.com/Zigres; **S. 3/ob. re.** Shutterstock.com/Olinchuk; **S. 3/ob.** Shutterstock.com/Anna Kutukova; **S. 4/un. mi.** Shutterstock.com/insta_photos; **S. 4/ob. mi.** Shutterstock.com/Antonio Guillem; **S. 4/mi.** Shutterstock.com/Lenar Nigmatullin; **S. 4/Zeichen** Cornelsen/D'avila Illustration Agency; **S. 4/Smileys** Shutterstock.com/Jan Engel; **S. 5/f** Shutterstock.com/MPH Photos; **S. 5/Handys** Shutterstock.com/Jeni Rodger; **S. 5/Wetterzeichen** Shutterstock.com/Sea Owl; **S. 5/c** Shutterstock.com/Matej Kastelic; **S. 5/a** Shutterstock.com/GaudiLab; **S. 5/un. re.** Shutterstock.com/Blaj Gabriel; **S. 5/d** Shutterstock.com/Monika Wisniewska; **S. 5/e** Shutterstock.com/Valery Sidelnykov; **S. 5/b** Shutterstock.com/Pressmaster; **S. 5/g** Shutterstock.com/Rainer Fuhrmann; **S. 6/3** Shutterstock.com/Anastasiia Horova; **S. 6/1** Shutterstock.com/Garfieldbigberm; **S. 6/un. re.** Shutterstock.com/Rido; **S. 6/ob.** Shutterstock.com/YAKOBCHUK VIACHESLAV; **S. 6/2** Shutterstock.com/thaikrit; **S. 6/4** Shutterstock.com/Jacqui Martin; **S. 6/5** Shutterstock.com/DOME STUDIO; **S. 6/un. li.** Cornelsen/D'avila Illustration Agency; **S. 7/Wetterzeichen** Shutterstock.com/Sea Owl; **S. 7/ob. li.** Shutterstock.com/StockImageFactory.com; **S. 7/un. mi.** Cornelsen/D'avila Illustration Agency; **S. 7/Musik** Shutterstock.com/Alexander Lysenko; **S. 7/Pizza** Shutterstock.com/Mochipet; **S. 7/Controller** Shutterstock.com/Mr.Creative; **S. 8/ob. re.** Shutterstock.com/StockImageFactory.com; **S. 8/ob. li.** Shutterstock.com/Iakov Filimonov; **S. 8/mi. re.** Shutterstock.com/Dean Drobot; **S. 8/ob. mi.** Shutterstock.com/Iakov Filimonov; **S. 9/li.** Shutterstock.com/StockImageFactory.com; **S. 9/mi.** Shutterstock.com/Olena Yakobchuk; **S. 9/re.** Shutterstock.com/Stephen Rees; **S. 10/ob.** Shutterstock.com/Pressmaster; **S. 10/un.** Cornelsen/D'avila Illustration Agency; **S. 11/mi.** Shutterstock.com/StockImageFactory.com; **S. 11/mi. li.** Shutterstock.com/StockImageFactory.com; **S. 11/ob. re.** Shutterstock.com/StockImageFactory.com; **S. 11/ob. li.** Shutterstock.com/StockImageFactory.com; **S. 11/mi. re.** Shutterstock.com/StockImageFactory.com; **S. 11/un.** Shutterstock.com/Rawpixel.com; **S. 11/ob. mi.** Shutterstock.com/Elenamiv; **S. 12/ob.** Shutterstock.com/TommyStockProject; **S. 12/2. Reihe li.** Shutterstock.com/November27; **S. 12/3. Reihe re.** Shutterstock.com/TAGSTOCK1; **S. 12/2. Reihe re.** Shutterstock.com/Africa Studio; **S. 12/3. Reihe li.** Shutterstock.com/DMegias; **S. 12/4. Reihe li.** Shutterstock.com/New Africa; **S. 12/4. Reihe re.** Shutterstock.com/javi_indy; **S. 12/un. li.** Shutterstock.com/stockfour; **S. 12/un. re.** Shutterstock.com/stockfour; **S. 14/café** Shutterstock.com/javi_indy; **S. 14/chess** Shutterstock.com/ideyweb; **S. 14/cinema** Shutterstock.com/Serhii Bobyk; **S. 14/fitness club** Shutterstock.com/antoniodiaz; **S. 14/park** Shutterstock.com/Syda Productions; **S. 14/stadium** Shutterstock.com/Altrendo Images; **S. 14/supermarket** Shutterstock.com/Monkey Business Images; **S. 14/swimming pool** Shutterstock.com/wavebreakmedia; **S. 14/un. li.** Shutterstock.com/MediaGroup_BestForYou; **S. 14/un. re.** Shutterstock.com/YAKOBCHUK VIACHESLAV; **S. 14/work out** Shutterstock.com/maxim4art; **S. 15/mi. li.** Shutterstock.com/SeventyFour; **S. 15/mi. re.** Shutterstock.com/M.Stasy; **S. 15/un.** Cornelsen/D'avila Illustration Agency; **S. 16/1** Shutterstock.com/Iryna Inshyna; **S. 16/2** Shutterstock.com/sirtravelalot; **S. 16/3** Shutterstock.com/WAYHOME studio; **S. 16/un.** Shutterstock.com/StockImageFactory.com; **S. 17/ob.** Shutterstock.com/Flamingo Images; **S. 17/un. li.** Shutterstock.com/Shane White; **S. 18/a** Shutterstock.com/Daniel M Ernst; **S. 18/b** Shutterstock.com/stockfour; **S. 18/c** Shutterstock.com/Xseon; **S. 18/d** Shutterstock.com/NattapolStudiO; **S. 18/Leroy** Shutterstock.com/Andrey_Popov; **S. 18/Mila** Shutterstock.com/WAYHOME studio; **S. 18/Walid** Shutterstock.com/Ebtikar; **S. 18/Ying** Shutterstock.com/EverGrump; **S. 19/ob. re.** Shutterstock.com/WAYHOME studio; **S. 19/Smileys** Shutterstock.com/Jan Engel; **S. 19/un.** Shutterstock.com/WAYHOME studio; **S. 19/Wetterzeichen** Shutterstock.com/Raura7; **S. 20/clever** Shutterstock.com/stockfour; **S. 20/freindly** Shutterstock.com/Ebtikar; **S. 20/funny** Shutterstock.com/Jacob Lund; **S. 20/helpful** Shutterstock.com/Iryna Inshyna; **S. 20/un. re.** Shutterstock.com/Corepics VOF; **S. 21/Apfel** Shutterstock.com/Tim UR; **S. 21/Banane** Shutterstock.com/bergamont; **S. 21/Birne** Shutterstock.com/bergamont; **S. 21/Bohne** Shutterstock.com/WIPHARAT CHAINUPAPHA; **S. 21/Kartoffel** Shutterstock.com/Flower Studio; **S. 21/Möhre** Shutterstock.com/Valentina Razumova; **S. 21/Orange** Shutterstock.com/Maks Narodenko; **S. 21/Tomate** Shutterstock.com/Tim UR; **S. 21/un. li.** Shutterstock.com/Macrovector; **S. 21/un. re.** Shutterstock.com/StockImageFactory.com; **S. 21/Zitrone** Shutterstock.com/Ian 2010; **S. 21/Zwiebel** Shutterstock.com/Kraichet chomchoey; **S. 22/ un. 2. v. li.** Shutterstock.com/airdone; **S. 22/Gendersymbole** Shutterstock.com/Uswa KDT; **S. 22/mi.** Shutterstock.com/fizkes; **S. 22/mi.** Shutterstock.com/fizkes; **S. 22/ob. li.** Shutterstock.com/StockImageFactory.com; **S. 22/ob. re.** Shutterstock.com/pukao; **S. 22/un. 1. v. li.** Shutterstock.com/Rido; **S. 22/un. 1. v. re.** Shutterstock.com/Life_imageS; **S. 22/un. 3. v. li.** Shutterstock.com/Drazen Zigic; **S. 23/a** Shutterstock.com/beats1; **S. 23/b** Shutterstock.com/Joshua Resnick; **S. 23/b** Shutterstock.com/Sura Nualpradid; **S. 23/Basam** Shutterstock.com/Ebtikar; **S. 23/bundi laddu** Shutterstock.com/Indian Creations; **S. 23/Chris** Shutterstock.com/mimagephotography; **S. 23/d** Shutterstock.com/MaraZe; **S. 23/Katja** Shutterstock.com/fizkes; **S. 23/un. re.** Shutterstock.com/StockImageFactory.com; **S. 23/Yaa** Shutterstock.com/mimagephotography; **S. 24/butter** Shutterstock.com/Zern Liew; **S. 24/chocolate** Shutterstock.com/Mironova Iuliia; **S. 24/eggs** Shutterstock.com/ID-EasyDoor; **S. 24/flour** Shutterstock.com/BlueRingMedia; **S. 24/milk** Shutterstock.com/Dacian G; **S. 24/ob. li.** Shutterstock.com/YAKOBCHUK VIACHESLAV; **S. 24/ob. re.** Shutterstock.com/StockImageFactory.com; **S. 24/sugar** Shutterstock.com/Zern Liew; **S. 25/mi.** Cornelsen/D'avila Illustration Agency; **S. 25/ob. li.** Shutterstock.com/ESB Basic; **S. 25/ob. re.** Shutterstock.com/StockImageFactory.com; **S. 25/un.** Shutterstock.com/BrunoRosa; **S. 26/butter** Shutterstock.com/BlueRingMedia; **S. 26/coins** Shutterstock.com/Claudio Divizia; **S. 26/eggs** Shutterstock.com/ID-EasyDoor; **S. 26/mi.** Shutterstock.com/StockImageFactory.com; **S. 26/notes** Shutterstock.com/kamui29; **S. 26/ob. li.** Shutterstock.com/Jane Kelly; **S. 26/ob. mi.** Shutterstock.com/Oakview Studios; **S. 26/ob. re.** Shutterstock.com/Pe3k; **S. 26/rice** Shutterstock.com/Gulyash; **S. 26/sugar** Shutterstock.com/Zern Liew; **S. 26/un. re.** Shutterstock.com/StockImageFactory.com; **S. 26/vegetables** Shutterstock.com/Alexander Raths; **S. 27/bread** Shutterstock.com/Sabelskaya; **S. 27/cakes** Shutterstock.com/andreysharonov; **S. 27/ob. re.** Shutterstock.com/Iakov Filimonov; **S. 27/un.** Shutterstock.com/ProStockStudio; **S. 28/a** Shutterstock.com/Africa Studio; **S. 28/b** Shutterstock.com/Africa Studio; **S. 28/c** Shutterstock.com/trevorb; **S. 28/d** Shutterstock.com/Africa Studio; **S. 28/f** Shutterstock.com/Uryupina Nadezhda; **S. 28/mi. re.** Shutterstock.com/StockImageFactory.com; **S. 28/pan** Shutterstock.com/DmitrievaLidiya; **S. 28/un. 1. v. li.** Shutterstock.com/Inga Nielsen; **S. 28/un. 1. v. re.** Shutterstock.com/Volodymyr Nik; **S. 28/un. 2. v. li.** Shutterstock.com/SOROKAJPG; **S. 28/un. 3. v. li.** Shutterstock.com/Smoczyslaw; **S. 29/a** Shutterstock.com/norikko; **S. 29/b** Shutterstock.com/Dariia Belkina; **S. 29/c** Shutterstock.com/Brent Hofacker; **S. 29/d** Shutterstock.com/Natalia Van Doninck; **S. 29/e** Shutterstock.com/Ana Flasker; **S. 29/f** Shutterstock.com/Francesco83; **S. 29/g** Shutterstock.com/Cristina.A; **S. 29/h** Shutterstock.com/Mahi ryan; **S. 29/jam** Shutterstock.com/Alter-ego; **S. 29/maple syrup** Shutterstock.com/Dancake; **S. 29/raisins** Shutterstock.com/NIPAPORN PANYACHAROEN; **S. 29/swette-savoury** Shutterstock.com/component; **S. 29/tasty** Shutterstock.com/Koltukovs; **S. 29/un. li.** Shutterstock.com/StockImageFactory.com; **S. 29/un. re.** Shutterstock.com/GaudiLab; **S. 30/barbecue** Shutterstock.com/stockcreations; **S. 30/bonfire** Shutterstock.com/Valeriy Karpeev; **S. 30/candle** Shutterstock.com/Mega Pixel; **S. 30/fireworks** Shutterstock.com/Steve Allen; **S. 30/ob. Cornelsen/D'avila Illustration Agency; S. 30/tree** Shutterstock.com/ajdebre; **S. 31/1. Reihe 1. v. li.** Shutterstock.com/Evgeny Atamanenko; **S. 31/1. Reihe 1. v. re.** Shutterstock.com/JessicaGirvan; **S. 31/1. Reihe 2. v. li.** Shutterstock.com/Mutaborr; **S. 31/1. Reihe 3. v. li.** Shutterstock.com/Impact Photography; **S. 31/2. Reihe 1. v. l.** Shutterstock.com/Monkey Business Images; **S. 31/2. Reihe 1. v. re.** Shutterstock.com/Radoslav Cajkovic; **S. 31/2. Reihe 2. v. li.** Shutterstock.com/Steve Allen; **S. 31/un. li.** Shutterstock.com/YAKOBCHUK VIACHESLAV; **S. 31/un. mi.** Shutterstock.com/Impact Photography; **S. 31/un. mi.** Shutterstock.com/salajean; **S. 31/un. re.** Shutterstock.com/Bikeworldtravel; **S. 32/mi. li.** Shutterstock.com/LightField Studios; **S. 32/mi. re.** Shutterstock.com/LightField Studios; **S. 32/mi.** Shutterstock.com/StockImageFactory.com; **S. 32/ob. li.** Shutterstock.com/StockImageFactory.com; **S. 32/ob. mi.** Shutterstock.com/StockImageFactory.com; **S. 33/1. Reihe li.** Shutterstock.com/YAKOBCHUK VIACHESLAV; **S. 33/1. Reihe re.** Shutterstock.com/StockImageFactory.com;

S. 33/2. Reihe 2. v. li. Shutterstock.com/David Soanes; **S. 33/2. Reihe 3. v. li.** Shutterstock.com/StockImageFactory.com; **S. 33/2. Reihe li.** Shutterstock.com/StockImageFactory.com; **S. 33/2. Reihe re.** Shutterstock.com/StockImageFactory.com; **S. 33/3. Reihe li.** Shutterstock.com/Fabian Junge; **S. 33/3. Reihe mi.** Shutterstock.com/Thierry Maffeis; **S. 33/3. Reihe re.** Shutterstock.com/Ezume Images; **S. 33/un.** Shutterstock.com/fizkes; **S. 34/li.** Shutterstock.com/JaneHYork; **S. 34/mi.** Shutterstock.com/Michael Conrad; **S. 34/ob. re.** Shutterstock.com/StockImageFactory.com; **S. 34/un.** Cornelsen/D'avila Illustration Agency; **S. 34/un. li.** Shutterstock.com/StockImageFactory.com; **S. 35/mi. li.** Shutterstock.com/Dmitry Naumov; **S. 35/mi. re.** Shutterstock.com/Borka Kiss; **S. 35/ob. li.** Shutterstock.com/StockImageFactory.com; **S. 35/ob. re.** Shutterstock.com/StockImageFactory.com; **S. 35/Symbole** Cornelsen/D'avila Illustration Agency; **S. 35/un.** Shutterstock.com/Yolanta; **S. 35/un. li.** Shutterstock.com/Radiokafka; **S. 36/bike** Shutterstock.com/GoodStudio; **S. 36/bus** Shutterstock.com/alazur; **S. 36/car** Shutterstock.com/Igogosha; **S. 36/ob. li.** Shutterstock.com/Rawpixel.com; **S. 36/ob. re.** Shutterstock.com/StockImageFactory.com; **S. 36/plane** Shutterstock.com/Janos Levente; **S. 36/train** Shutterstock.com/CK Singh; **S. 37/un. li.** Shutterstock.com/F8 Studio; **S. 37/un. re.** Shutterstock.com/VGstockstudio; **S. 37/mi. re.** Shutterstock.com/Keith Gentry; **S. 37/un. mi.** Shutterstock.com/Dasha Rosato; **S. 38/Apartement** Shutterstock.com/Photographee.eu; **S. 38/Buckingham Palace** Shutterstock.com/maziarz; **S. 38/Bus Tour** Shutterstock.com/Richie Chan; **S. 38/cook at home** Shutterstock.com/Skylines; **S. 38/East end Hotel** Shutterstock.com/Elnur; **S. 38/Fish and Ships** Shutterstock.com/Paul Cowan; **S. 38/Hotel Victoria** Shutterstock.com/vvoe; **S. 38/indian restaurant** Shutterstock.com/Finn stock; **S. 38/London Eye** Shutterstock.com/QQ7; **S. 38/ob. re.** Shutterstock.com/Ole Hartvig; **S. 39/li.** Shutterstock.com/Prostock-studio; **S. 39/mi.** Shutterstock.com/grum; **S. 39/re.** Shutterstock.com/Carolina Arroyo; **S. 40/feta salad** Shutterstock.com/Anton Starikov; **S. 40/mi. li.** Shutterstock.com/Tirachard Kumtanom; **S. 40/ob. re.** Shutterstock.com/VGstockstudio; **S. 40/un. li.** Shutterstock.com/michaeljung; **S. 40/un. re.** Shutterstock.com/sirtravelalot; **S. 41/ob.** Cornelsen/D'avila Illustration Agency; **S. 41/tools** Shutterstock.com/mihalec; **S. 41/truck** Shutterstock.com/ideyweb; **S. 41/van** Shutterstock.com/Zhenyakot; **S. 42/1** Shutterstock.com/wavebreakmedia; **S. 42/2** Shutterstock.com/George Rudy; **S. 42/3** Shutterstock.com/Monkey Business Images; **S. 42/4** Shutterstock.com/antoniodiaz; **S. 42/5** Shutterstock.com/Prostock-studio; **S. 42/6** Shutterstock.com/Fernando Avendano; **S. 43/mi. li.** Shutterstock.com/StockImageFactory.com; **S. 43/ob. li.** Shutterstock.com/YAKOBCHUK VIACHESLAV; **S. 43/ob. re.** Shutterstock.com/StockImageFactory.com; **S. 43/un.** Shutterstock.com/garetsworkshop; **S. 44/comic** Cornelsen/D'avila Illustration Agency; **S. 44/ob. li.** Shutterstock.com/StockImageFactory.com; **S. 46/blouse** Shutterstock.com/pornpawit; **S. 46/mi. li.** Shutterstock.com/Anton Gvozdikov; **S. 46/mi. re.** Shutterstock.com/Pressmaster; **S. 46/ob. li.** Shutterstock.com/sirtravelalot; **S. 46/ob. re.** Shutterstock.com/Pressmaster; **S. 46/serviettes** Shutterstock.com/bigacis; **S. 47/corner** Shutterstock.com/montego; **S. 47/cupboard** Shutterstock.com/chaiwatartwork; **S. 47/ob. li.** Shutterstock.com/fizkes; **S. 47/ob. re.** Shutterstock.com/StockImageFactory.com; **S. 47/photocopier** Shutterstock.com/MicroOne; **S. 47/un.** Cornelsen/D'avila Illustration Agency; **S. 48/** Cornelsen/D'avila Illustration Agency; **S. 48/key** Shutterstock.com/Gavran333; **S. 48/mi. li.** Shutterstock.com/stockfour; **S. 48/Symbols** Cornelsen/D'avila Illustration Agency; **S. 49/alle** Cornelsen/D'avila Illustration Agency; **S. 50/Symbols** Cornelsen/D'avila Illustration Agency; **S. 50/un.** Shutterstock.com/fizkes; **S. 51/Amira** Shutterstock.com/StockImageFactory.com; **S. 51/Farah** Shutterstock.com/Rido; **S. 51/ob. mi.** Shutterstock.com/Daniel M Ernst; **S. 51/Ollie** Shutterstock.com/YAKOBCHUK VIACHESLAV; **S. 51/Rahul** Shutterstock.com/StockImageFactory.com; **S. 51/Tayo** Shutterstock.com/YAKOBCHUK VIACHESLAV; **S. 51/un. li.** Shutterstock.com/Daniel M Ernst; **S. 52/ob. re.** Shutterstock.com/StockImageFactory.com; **S. 52/un. re.** Shutterstock.com/StockImageFactory.com; **S. 53/un.** Shutterstock.com/wavebreakmedia; **S. 54/mi. re.** Shutterstock.com/YAKOBCHUK VIACHESLAV; **S. 54/ob. re.** Shutterstock.com/StockImageFactory.com; **S. 56/Adu** Shutterstock.com/fizkes; **S. 56/Jack** Shutterstock/oliveromg; **S. 56/Kim** Shutterstock.com/Dragon Images; **S. 56/Lang** Shutterstock.com/PR Image Factory; **S. 56/un. re.** Shutterstock.com/StockImageFactory.com; **S. 57/ob. re.** Shutterstock.com/StockImageFactory.com; **S. 59/ob. li.** Shutterstock.com/StockImageFactory.com; **S. 60/mi. li.** Shutterstock.com/StockImageFactory.com; **S. 60/mi. re.** Shutterstock.com/StockImageFactory.com; **S. 60/ob. li.** Shutterstock.com/StockImageFactory.com; **S. 60/ob. re.** Shutterstock.com/StockImageFactory.com; **S. 61/mi. re.** Shutterstock.com/Pixel-Shot; **S. 61/ob. re.** Shutterstock.com/BAZA Production; **S. 61/un. re.** Shutterstock.com/AJR_photo; **S. 62/coins** Shutterstock.com/Claudio Divizia; **S. 62/dice** Shutterstock.com/Stock Ninja Studio; **S. 63/1. v. ob. re.** Shutterstock.com/Antonio Guillem; **S. 63/2. v. ob. re.** Shutterstock.com/Lenar Nigmatullin; **S. 63/3. v. ob. re.** Shutterstock.com/insta_photos; **S. 63/un. li.** Shutterstock.com/YAKOBCHUK VIACHESLAV; **S. 63/un. re.** Shutterstock.com/YAKOBCHUK VIACHESLAV; **S. 64/mi.** Shutterstock.com/Iakov Filimonov; **S. 65/re.** Shutterstock.com/YAKOBCHUK VIACHESLAV; **S. 66/mi. li.** Shutterstock.com/Iryna Inshyna; **S. 66/ob. re.** Shutterstock.com/WAYHOME studio; **S. 66/un. re.** Shutterstock.com/sirtravelalot; **S. 67/Basam** Shutterstock.com/Ebtikar; **S. 67/Chris** Shutterstock.com/mimagephotography; **S. 67/Katja** Shutterstock.com/fizkes; **S. 67/Yaa** Shutterstock.com/mimagephotography; **S. 68/ob. re.** Shutterstock.com/Iakov Filimonov; **S. 68/un. li.** Shutterstock.com/YAKOBCHUK VIACHESLAV; **S. 68/un. mi.** Shutterstock.com/Impact Photography; **S. 68/un. mi.** Shutterstock.com/salajean; **S. 68/un. re.** Shutterstock.com/Bikeworldtravel; **S. 69/Dublin Castle** Shutterstock.com/Fabian Junge; **S. 69/Irish Stew** Shutterstock.com/Ezume Images; **S. 69/River Liffey** Shutterstock.com/David Soanes; **S. 69/un. re.** Shutterstock.com/Keith Gentry; **S. 70/1** Shutterstock.com/sirtravelalot; **S. 70/2** Shutterstock.com/Anton Gvozdikov; **S. 70/3** Shutterstock.com/Pressmaster; **S. 70/4** Shutterstock.com/Pressmaster; **S. 70/mi. li.** Shutterstock.com/StockImageFactory.com; **S. 70/mi. re.** Shutterstock.com/StockImageFactory.com; **S. 70/ob. li.** Shutterstock.com/YAKOBCHUK VIACHESLAV; **S. 71/mi. re.** Shutterstock.com/StockImageFactory.com; **S. 71/un. re.** Shutterstock.com/StockImageFactory.com;